Flourish in Life

Proven Methods to Enhance Your Personal Growth and Well-being

Rachel Byrd

© Copyright 2024 by Rachel Byrd
All Rights Reserved

The presentation of the information is without contract or any type of guarantee assurance. The trademarks that are used are without any consent, and the publication of the trademark is without permission or backing by the trademark owner. All trademarks and brands within this book are for clarifying purposes only and are the owned by the owners themselves, not affiliated with this document.

Table of Contents

Chapter 1

ntroduction The Journey to Flourishing

What Does It Mean to Flourish?

Flourishing is a concept that transcends mere survival or the pursuit of happiness; it is about achieving a state of optimal functioning and well-being. To flourish means to grow vigorously, to thrive, and to be in a state where one's potential is fully realized. This idea is rooted in positive psychology, a field that examines what makes life worth living and how individuals can lead fulfilling lives. Flourishing is not just about feeling good but also about doing good and being good. It is a holistic state that encompasses emotional, psychological, and social well-being, allowing individuals to function at their best.

At its core, flourishing involves a deep sense of purpose and meaning. It is about understanding one's values and aligning one's actions with those values. When people have a clear sense of why they are doing what they are doing, they are more likely to experience a sense of fulfillment and satisfaction. This sense of purpose acts as a guiding star, helping individuals navigate through life's challenges and obstacles with resilience and determination.

Flourishing also involves the cultivation of positive emotions. While negative emotions are a natural part of the human experience, flourishing individuals tend to experience a higher ratio of positive to negative emotions. This doesn't mean they are always happy or that they never feel sad or angry. Instead, they have developed the skills to manage their emotions effectively and to bounce back from adversity. Positive emotions such as joy, gratitude, and love can broaden one's perspective and build psychological resources, making it easier to cope with stress and setbacks.

Another key component of flourishing is the development of strong, supportive relationships. Human beings are inherently social creatures, and our relationships play a crucial role in our overall well-being. Flourishing individuals invest time and effort into building and maintaining healthy relationships with family, friends, and colleagues. These relationships provide a sense of belonging and support, which can buffer against the negative effects of stress and promote a sense of security and stability.

Engagement is another essential aspect of flourishing. This involves being fully absorbed and present in the activities one is involved in, whether it be work, hobbies, or personal interests. When individuals are engaged, they enter a state of flow, where they lose track of time and become completely immersed in what they are doing. This state of deep involvement and concentration can lead to a sense of accomplishment and fulfillment.

Flourishing also requires the cultivation of personal strengths and virtues. This involves recognizing and developing one's unique talents and abilities and using them in ways that contribute to the greater good. When individuals use their strengths, they are more likely to experience a sense of competence and mastery, which can boost their self-esteem and overall well-being. Additionally, practicing virtues such as kindness, generosity, and integrity can enhance one's sense of moral and ethical fulfillment.

A flourishing life is also characterized by a sense of autonomy and control. This means having the ability to make choices and take actions that are consistent with one's values and goals. When individuals feel that they have control over their lives and are able to influence their circumstances, they are more likely to experience a sense of empowerment and motivation. This sense of control can also reduce feelings of helplessness and increase one's ability to cope with challenges.

Resilience is another important component of flourishing. This refers to the ability to bounce back from adversity and to adapt to difficult situations. Resilient individuals view challenges as opportunities for growth and learning rather than as insurmountable obstacles. They have developed coping strategies that allow them to manage stress effectively and to maintain a positive outlook even in the face of setbacks. Building resilience involves developing a growth mindset, where one views failures as temporary and as opportunities for improvement.

Flourishing also involves the pursuit of meaningful goals. These are goals that are aligned with one's values and that contribute to a sense of purpose and direction in life. When individuals set and work towards meaningful goals, they are more likely to experience a sense of progress and achievement. This sense of accomplishment can enhance one's overall well-being and provide motivation to continue striving for personal growth and development.

Physical well-being is another important aspect of flourishing. This involves taking care of one's body through proper nutrition, regular exercise, and adequate sleep. Physical health is closely linked to emotional and psychological well-being, and maintaining a healthy lifestyle can enhance one's overall sense of vitality and energy. When individuals prioritize their physical health, they are better equipped to handle stress and to engage in activities that promote personal growth and well-being.

Finally, flourishing involves a sense of balance and harmony. This means finding a healthy equilibrium between different areas of one's life, such as work, family, and personal interests. When individuals are able to balance their responsibilities and activities, they are more likely to experience a sense of stability and satisfaction. Achieving balance requires setting priorities, managing one's time effectively, and being mindful of one's needs and well-being.

The Importance of Personal Growth

Personal growth is the ongoing process of understanding and developing oneself in order to achieve one's fullest potential. It is an essential part of human development and involves a deep, lifelong commitment to self-improvement, learning, and personal transformation. The importance of personal growth cannot be overstated, as it impacts every aspect of our lives, from our relationships and careers to our mental health and overall well-being.

At its core, personal growth is about becoming the best version of yourself. This journey begins with self-awareness, the ability to reflect on your thoughts, emotions, and behaviors and understand how they influence your life. Self-awareness is the foundation upon which personal growth is built. It allows you to recognize your strengths and weaknesses, understand your values and beliefs, and identify the areas of your life that need improvement.

One of the primary reasons personal growth is so important is that it leads to greater self-confidence and self-esteem. As you work on developing your skills, knowledge, and abilities, you begin to see tangible improvements in your life. These achievements, no matter how small, contribute to a growing sense of self-worth and confidence. When you believe in your own capabilities, you are more likely to take on new challenges and pursue opportunities that you might have otherwise avoided.

Personal growth also plays a crucial role in building resilience. Life is full of challenges, setbacks, and unexpected events. How you respond to these situations often depends on your level of personal development. Resilient individuals are better equipped to handle stress, adapt to change, and bounce back from adversity. They view challenges as opportunities for growth rather than insurmountable obstacles. This mindset allows them to navigate life's ups and downs with greater ease and stability.

Another significant benefit of personal growth is improved relationships. As you become more self-aware and emotionally intelligent, you are better able to understand and manage your own emotions. This, in turn, allows you to communicate more effectively, empathize with others, and build stronger, healthier relationships. Personal growth helps you develop the skills needed to navigate conflicts, set healthy boundaries, and foster genuine connections with those around you.

Personal growth is also closely linked to professional success. In today's fast-paced, ever-changing world, the ability to continuously learn and adapt is essential. Those who commit to personal growth are more likely to stay current with industry trends, develop new skills, and seize opportunities for career advancement. Employers value individuals who demonstrate a commitment to self-improvement and a willingness to take on new challenges. By investing in your personal growth, you increase your value in the workplace and open up new possibilities for professional development.

Furthermore, personal growth is integral to achieving a sense of purpose and fulfillment. Many people go through life feeling unfulfilled or disconnected, often because they have not taken the time to explore their passions, values, and goals. Personal growth encourages you to delve deep into these areas, helping you to uncover what truly matters to you. This process of self-discovery can lead to a more meaningful and purpose-driven life. When you align your actions with your values and pursue goals that resonate with your true self, you experience a greater sense of satisfaction and fulfillment.

Personal growth also has a profound impact on mental health and well-being. Engaging in activities that promote self-improvement, such as mindfulness, meditation, and regular physical exercise, can reduce stress, anxiety, and depression. These practices help to create a positive mindset and foster a sense of inner peace and balance. Additionally, personal growth encourages healthy habits and behaviors, such as setting boundaries, practicing self-care, and seeking support when needed. These habits contribute to overall mental and emotional well-being, allowing you to lead a healthier, more balanced life.

A commitment to personal growth also fosters a sense of autonomy and control. When you take responsibility for your own development, you are actively shaping your future rather than passively reacting to circumstances. This sense of agency empowers you to make informed decisions, set and achieve meaningful goals, and take deliberate actions towards your desired outcomes. As a result, you feel more in control of your life and more confident in your ability to navigate its complexities.

Personal growth is not a destination but a continuous journey. It requires a mindset of lifelong learning and a willingness to embrace change. This journey is often challenging and requires effort and dedication, but the rewards are immeasurable. By committing to personal growth, you embark on a path of self-discovery, self-improvement, and self-fulfillment. You develop the skills, knowledge, and resilience needed to overcome obstacles, achieve your goals, and lead a more meaningful and fulfilling life.

Moreover, personal growth has a ripple effect that extends beyond the individual. As you grow and develop, you positively impact those around you. Your improved self-awareness, emotional intelligence, and communication skills enhance your interactions with others, fostering healthier and more supportive relationships. Your resilience and positive mindset inspire those around you to adopt similar attitudes. In this way, personal growth contributes not only to your own well-being but also to the well-being of your community and society as a whole.

To truly embrace personal growth, it is important to set clear, achievable goals and to create a plan for reaching them. This involves identifying the areas of your life that you want to improve, setting specific and measurable objectives, and taking consistent action towards achieving them. It is also important to regularly reflect on your progress and to adjust your plan as needed. This process of goal-setting and reflection helps to keep you focused and motivated on your journey of personal development.

Another key aspect of personal growth is seeking out opportunities for learning and development. This can involve formal education, such as taking courses or earning certifications, as well as informal learning, such as reading books, attending workshops, or seeking out mentors. Surrounding yourself with individuals who support and encourage your growth can also be incredibly beneficial. These individuals can provide valuable feedback, guidance, and

inspiration, helping you to stay motivated and on
track.

Setting the Foundation for Well-being

Setting the foundation for well-being starts with
understanding that well-being is a multifaceted
concept encompassing physical health, emotional
stability, social connections, and a sense of purpose.
Each of these components is essential to creating a
balanced and fulfilling life. By addressing each area
intentionally and thoughtfully, you lay the
groundwork for a resilient and thriving existence.

Physical health is often the most tangible aspect of
well-being, and it forms a crucial part of the
foundation. The body and mind are deeply
interconnected, and caring for your physical health
can lead to profound benefits for your emotional and
mental state. Regular exercise is a cornerstone of
physical health. It doesn't necessarily mean hitting the
gym every day but finding activities that you enjoy
and can stick with consistently. Whether it's a
morning jog, a session of yoga, or a dance class,
moving your body releases endorphins, reduces
stress, and improves overall mood.

Nutrition is another critical component. What you eat
fuels your body and mind, and making nutritious
choices can significantly impact your energy levels
and mental clarity. A balanced diet rich in fruits,
vegetables, lean proteins, and whole grains provides
the essential nutrients your body needs to function

optimally. Hydration is equally important; drinking enough water throughout the day keeps your body systems running smoothly and can even improve mood and cognitive function.

Sleep is often underestimated in its importance, yet it is fundamental to well-being. Quality sleep allows your body to repair itself, consolidate memories, and regulate emotions. Establishing a consistent sleep routine, creating a restful environment, and avoiding stimulants like caffeine or electronic screens before bed can significantly enhance the quality of your sleep.

Emotional stability forms the second pillar of well-being. It begins with self-awareness, understanding your emotions, and recognizing the triggers that affect your mood. Mindfulness practices, such as meditation or journaling, can help you stay present and manage your emotions more effectively. By reflecting on your thoughts and feelings, you develop a deeper understanding of yourself, which is crucial for emotional regulation.

Stress management is a critical aspect of emotional stability. Chronic stress can have detrimental effects on both your physical and mental health. Identifying stressors in your life and developing strategies to manage them is essential. Techniques such as deep breathing exercises, progressive muscle relaxation, or engaging in hobbies can provide relief. It's also important to set realistic expectations and learn to say no when necessary, ensuring that you do not overextend yourself.

Building resilience is another key factor. Resilience is the ability to bounce back from setbacks and adapt to challenges. Cultivating a growth mindset, where you view difficulties as opportunities for learning and growth, can enhance your resilience. Surrounding yourself with supportive relationships and seeking help when needed also contribute to your ability to cope with adversity.

Social connections form the third essential pillar of well-being. Human beings are inherently social creatures, and the quality of our relationships has a profound impact on our happiness and health. Nurturing deep, meaningful relationships with family, friends, and community provides a sense of belonging and support. These connections offer emotional support, practical assistance, and a sense of shared purpose.

Effective communication is vital for building and maintaining these relationships. Active listening, empathy, and expressing your thoughts and feelings honestly and respectfully help foster strong connections. It's also important to invest time and energy into your relationships, making an effort to stay connected and show appreciation for the people in your life.

Building a sense of community extends beyond personal relationships. Engaging in social activities, volunteering, or joining clubs and organizations can provide a broader sense of connection and purpose. These activities not only offer opportunities for social interaction but also allow you to contribute to something larger than yourself, enhancing your overall sense of well-being.

The final pillar of well-being is having a sense of purpose. Purpose gives direction and meaning to your life, motivating you to pursue goals and engage in activities that align with your values and passions. Identifying your purpose begins with introspection—reflecting on your interests, strengths, and what you find fulfilling. Setting goals that are meaningful to you and taking steps towards achieving them can provide a sense of accomplishment and direction.

It's important to recognize that your purpose can evolve over time. Life experiences, personal growth, and changing circumstances can all influence your sense of purpose. Being open to this evolution and continuously seeking activities and goals that resonate with you can help maintain a sense of fulfillment.

Combining these four pillars—physical health, emotional stability, social connections, and a sense of purpose—creates a holistic approach to well-being. Each pillar supports and enhances the others, contributing to a balanced and resilient foundation. By addressing each area intentionally, you can create a life that is not only healthier but also more meaningful and satisfying.

Implementing changes to set this foundation can be challenging, but starting small and being consistent is key. Begin by identifying one or two areas that you feel need the most attention and focus on making gradual improvements. Celebrate your successes, no matter how small, and be patient with yourself as you work towards a more balanced and fulfilling life.

For instance, if physical health is an area you want to improve, start by incorporating short walks into your daily routine or making one healthy dietary change at a time. If emotional stability is your focus, try setting aside a few minutes each day for mindfulness practice or journaling. For social connections, consider reaching out to a friend you haven't spoken to in a while or joining a local group that interests you. If you are seeking purpose, spend time reflecting on what activities bring you joy and fulfillment and explore ways to incorporate more of those into your life.

It's also important to regularly assess your progress and make adjustments as needed. Life is dynamic, and your needs and circumstances will change over time. Periodically reviewing your goals and practices ensures that you remain aligned with your current situation and continue to build on your foundation for well-being.

How to Use This Book

Books can be powerful tools for learning and personal growth, but their true value is realized only when you know how to use them effectively. This book is designed to guide you on a journey of self-improvement, providing practical advice, exercises, and insights to help you achieve your goals. To make the most of this book, it's important to understand its structure, how to approach its content, and how to integrate the lessons into your everyday life.

First, let's talk about the structure of the book. Each chapter is carefully crafted to cover a specific aspect of personal development, offering a blend of theory and practice. The chapters build on each other, taking you from foundational concepts to more advanced techniques. While the book is designed to be read sequentially, you can also jump to the chapters that resonate most with your current needs. However, for a comprehensive understanding, it's beneficial to follow the order as each chapter lays the groundwork for the next.

As you read, it's crucial to engage actively with the material. Passive reading might provide some insights, but true growth comes from applying what you learn. Take notes, highlight key points, and reflect on how the concepts relate to your life. Consider keeping a journal specifically for this book, where you can jot down thoughts, questions, and reflections. This practice not only helps reinforce your learning but also allows you to track your progress over time.

Incorporating the exercises and activities presented in the book is essential for translating theory into practice. These exercises are designed to help you internalize the concepts and see real changes in your life. Approach each exercise with an open mind and a willingness to experiment. Some activities might push you out of your comfort zone, but that's where growth happens. Commit to doing the exercises consistently, even if they feel challenging at first. Over time, you'll find that they become easier and more natural.

One effective way to use this book is by setting aside dedicated time each day or week to focus on it. Treat this time as an important appointment with yourself, free from distractions. Consistency is key to building new habits and making lasting changes. Whether it's 15 minutes a day or an hour a week, find a routine that works for you and stick to it. This regular practice will help reinforce the concepts and ensure that you're making steady progress.

Another important aspect of using this book effectively is to be patient and kind to yourself. Personal development is a journey, and it's natural to encounter setbacks or periods of slow progress. Don't be discouraged if you don't see immediate results. Remember, the goal is not perfection but continuous improvement. Celebrate your small victories along the way and learn from your mistakes. Over time, these small steps will accumulate into significant changes.

Sharing your journey with others can also enhance your experience. Consider discussing the book with a friend or joining a study group. Sharing insights, challenges, and successes can provide additional motivation and accountability. It can also offer new perspectives and deepen your understanding of the material. If you prefer, you can also seek out online communities or forums where you can connect with others who are reading the same book.

Applying the lessons from the book to real-life situations is where the true transformation happens. As you go through your daily life, look for opportunities to practice what you've learned. Whether it's using a new communication technique in a conversation, applying a stress management strategy during a hectic day, or setting a personal goal and working towards it, integrating the lessons into your life is crucial. The more you practice, the more these new skills and habits will become a natural part of who you are.

Reflecting on your progress regularly is another important practice. Take time to review your notes and journal entries, and assess how far you've come. What changes have you noticed in your thoughts, behaviors, and emotions? What areas still need work? This reflection not only helps you recognize your achievements but also identifies areas for further growth. It's a valuable tool for staying on track and maintaining momentum.

Another tip for using this book effectively is to keep an open mind and be willing to adapt. Personal development is not a one-size-fits-all process. What works for one person might not work for another. Be willing to try different approaches and modify the exercises to suit your unique needs and circumstances. The book provides a framework, but you have the flexibility to tailor it to your personal journey.

Additionally, it's important to revisit the book periodically. As you grow and change, different chapters or sections might resonate with you in new ways. What seemed less relevant at one point might become more meaningful later on. Revisiting the material allows you to deepen your understanding and apply the concepts to new challenges and opportunities that arise in your life.

Lastly, remember that this book is just one tool among many. Personal development is a lifelong journey, and there are countless resources available to support you. Continue seeking out new knowledge, experiences, and perspectives. Combine the insights from this book with other books, courses, mentors, and life experiences. The more diverse your learning

sources, the richer your personal growth journey will
be.

A Roadmap to Personal Transformation

Embarking on a journey of personal transformation requires a well-thought-out roadmap. This chapter will provide you with a clear, actionable guide to help you achieve meaningful and lasting change in your life. The process involves self-discovery, goal setting, strategic planning, and continuous reflection and adjustment. By following this roadmap, you will be able to navigate the complexities of personal growth with greater clarity and confidence.

The first step in personal transformation is self-discovery. Understanding who you are, what you value, and what you aspire to become is foundational. Start by reflecting on your past experiences and identifying patterns in your behavior, thoughts, and emotions. Consider what activities make you feel energized and fulfilled and which ones drain you. Journaling can be a helpful tool in this process. Write about your experiences, your feelings, and your thoughts. Over time, you will start to see patterns and gain insights into your true self.

Once you have a clearer understanding of yourself, it's time to set goals. Effective goals are specific, measurable, achievable, relevant, and time-bound (SMART). Think about what you want to achieve in different areas of your life, such as your career, relationships, health, and personal development.

Write down your goals and ensure they align with your values and long-term vision. For example, if you value creativity and self-expression, a goal might be to start a blog or learn a new artistic skill.

With your goals in place, the next step is strategic planning. Break down each goal into smaller, manageable tasks. Create a timeline for each task and set deadlines to keep yourself accountable. It's important to be realistic about what you can achieve within a given timeframe. Overloading yourself with too many tasks can lead to burnout and frustration. Instead, focus on steady, consistent progress. Prioritize your tasks based on their importance and urgency. This will help you stay focused and ensure that you are making meaningful progress towards your goals.

As you begin to take action, it's crucial to maintain a positive mindset. Personal transformation is a challenging process, and setbacks are inevitable. Instead of viewing setbacks as failures, see them as opportunities for learning and growth. Cultivate resilience by practicing self-compassion and reminding yourself of your strengths and achievements. Surround yourself with supportive people who encourage and motivate you. Their positive influence can make a significant difference in your journey.

Another key aspect of personal transformation is continuous learning. Seek out new knowledge and experiences that can help you grow. Read books, attend workshops, take courses, and engage in activities that challenge you. This not only broadens your perspective but also equips you with new skills and insights. Be open to feedback and willing to adjust your approach based on what you learn. Personal transformation is an ongoing process, and there is always room for improvement.

To ensure that you stay on track, regularly review your progress. Set aside time each week or month to reflect on what you have achieved and what still needs work. Adjust your plans as necessary and celebrate your successes, no matter how small. This reflection helps you stay motivated and focused on your goals. It also allows you to identify any obstacles that may be hindering your progress and develop strategies to overcome them.

In addition to regular reviews, it's important to stay flexible and adaptable. Life is unpredictable, and circumstances can change. Being rigid in your approach can lead to frustration and stagnation. Instead, be open to modifying your goals and plans as needed. This flexibility allows you to navigate challenges more effectively and stay aligned with your overall vision.

One powerful tool for personal transformation is visualization. Spend time each day imagining yourself achieving your goals and living the life you desire. Visualization helps to reinforce your commitment and keeps you focused on your objectives. It can also boost your confidence and motivation by making your goals feel more attainable. Combine visualization with positive affirmations to further strengthen your mindset and belief in your ability to succeed.

Another important aspect of personal transformation is taking care of your physical and mental health. A healthy body and mind provide the foundation for all your efforts. Ensure that you are getting enough sleep, eating a balanced diet, and engaging in regular physical activity. Practice mindfulness and stress management techniques to maintain your mental well-being. When your body and mind are in good condition, you are better equipped to handle challenges and pursue your goals with vigor.

Building a support network is also crucial for personal transformation. Surround yourself with people who share your values and goals. Seek out mentors and role models who can provide guidance and inspiration. Engage in communities and groups that align with your interests and aspirations. These connections can offer valuable advice, encouragement, and accountability. They can also provide a sense of belonging and camaraderie, making your journey more enjoyable and fulfilling.

As you progress on your journey, it's important to give back and help others. Sharing your experiences and insights can inspire and motivate those around you. It also reinforces your own learning and growth. Volunteer your time, mentor others, and contribute to causes that are meaningful to you. Helping others not only makes a positive impact on their lives but also enriches your own personal transformation journey.

Finally, remember that personal transformation is a lifelong journey. There is no definitive endpoint, as growth and improvement are continuous processes. Embrace the journey with curiosity and enthusiasm. Celebrate your progress and be grateful for the opportunities to learn and evolve. Each step you take

brings you closer to becoming the best version of
yourself.

Chapter 2

Understanding Personal Growth

The Psychology of Personal Growth

Understanding the psychology of personal growth is fundamental to achieving lasting change and fulfillment. Personal growth is not just about setting goals and working hard to achieve them; it's about understanding the mental and emotional processes that drive your behaviors and decisions. By exploring these psychological aspects, you can develop a deeper awareness of your motivations, overcome obstacles, and create a sustainable path toward self-improvement.

Personal growth begins with self-awareness. Self-awareness involves recognizing your thoughts, emotions, and behaviors and understanding how they influence your life. It's about being honest with yourself regarding your strengths and weaknesses. One effective way to enhance self-awareness is through mindfulness practices. Mindfulness encourages you to stay present and observe your inner experiences without judgment. By regularly practicing mindfulness, you can gain insights into your habitual patterns and begin to make conscious choices rather than reacting automatically.

In addition to mindfulness, another tool for self-awareness is reflective journaling. Writing about your daily experiences, thoughts, and feelings helps you process and understand them better. It allows you to identify recurring themes or issues that may be affecting your growth. For instance, you might notice that you tend to avoid challenges due to a fear of failure. Recognizing this pattern is the first step toward addressing and overcoming it.

Once you have a clearer understanding of yourself, it's important to explore your motivations. Motivation is the driving force behind your actions and behaviors. Psychologists distinguish between intrinsic and extrinsic motivation. Intrinsic motivation comes from within and is driven by personal satisfaction and a sense of accomplishment. Extrinsic motivation, on the other hand, is driven by external rewards such as money, recognition, or approval from others. Research suggests that intrinsic motivation is more sustainable and leads to greater long-term satisfaction. Therefore, it's beneficial to align your personal growth goals with your intrinsic motivations. Ask yourself what truly excites and fulfills you, and focus on those areas.

Another crucial psychological concept in personal growth is self-efficacy, which is the belief in your ability to succeed in specific situations or accomplish a task. High self-efficacy can boost your confidence and resilience, making you more likely to take on challenges and persist in the face of obstacles. To enhance your self-efficacy, start by setting small, achievable goals. Success in these smaller tasks builds your confidence and prepares you for larger challenges. Additionally, seek out role models and mentors who can provide guidance and encouragement. Their support can reinforce your belief in your capabilities.

Mindset also plays a critical role in personal growth. Carol Dweck, a renowned psychologist, introduced the concept of fixed and growth mindsets. Individuals with a fixed mindset believe that their abilities and intelligence are static and unchangeable. In contrast, those with a growth mindset believe that they can develop their abilities through effort and learning. Adopting a growth mindset fosters resilience and a willingness to embrace challenges. To cultivate a growth mindset, focus on the process rather than the outcome. Celebrate your efforts and progress, and view failures as opportunities for learning and improvement.

Emotional intelligence is another key aspect of personal growth. Emotional intelligence involves recognizing, understanding, and managing your own emotions, as well as empathizing with others. High emotional intelligence can improve your relationships, reduce stress, and enhance your decision-making abilities. To develop emotional intelligence, practice active listening and empathy. Pay attention to the emotions of those around you and strive to understand their perspectives. Additionally, work on managing your own emotions by identifying triggers and developing healthy coping strategies.

The concept of resilience is closely tied to personal growth. Resilience is the ability to bounce back from adversity and maintain a positive outlook despite challenges. Building resilience involves developing a strong support network, maintaining a hopeful attitude, and practicing self-care. When faced with setbacks, focus on what you can control and take proactive steps to address the situation. Reflect on past experiences where you successfully overcame difficulties and draw strength from those memories.

Another important psychological principle in personal growth is the power of habits. Habits are automatic behaviors that are formed through repeated actions. They can either support or hinder your growth, depending on their nature. To develop positive habits, start by identifying the behaviors you want to change or establish. Break these behaviors into small, manageable steps and consistently practice them until they become ingrained. Use cues and rewards to reinforce the desired behavior. For example, if you want to develop a habit of exercising, set a specific time each day for your workout and reward yourself with something enjoyable afterward.

Cognitive-behavioral techniques can also be effective in personal growth. These techniques involve identifying and challenging negative thought patterns that may be holding you back. Cognitive restructuring, for instance, helps you reframe negative thoughts into more positive and constructive ones. If you catch yourself thinking, "I'll never be able to do this," challenge that thought by asking, "What evidence do I have for this belief? What can I do to improve my skills?" By shifting your mindset, you can reduce self-doubt and increase your motivation to pursue your goals.

Another psychological factor that influences personal growth is social comparison. While comparing yourself to others is natural, it can be detrimental if it leads to feelings of inadequacy or low self-esteem.

Instead of comparing yourself to others, focus on your own progress and achievements. Set personal benchmarks and celebrate your unique journey. Remember that everyone's path is different, and what matters most is your individual growth and fulfillment.

Finally, the role of purpose and meaning in personal growth cannot be overstated. Having a clear sense of purpose provides direction and motivation. It gives you a reason to persevere through challenges and setbacks. To discover your purpose, reflect on what matters most to you and how you can contribute to something larger than yourself. Consider your passions, values, and strengths, and think about how you can use them to make a positive impact. Pursuing a purpose-driven life can lead to greater satisfaction and a deeper sense of fulfillment.

Identifying Your Strengths and Weaknesses

Recognizing your strengths and weaknesses is a crucial step in the journey of personal growth. It begins with deep self-reflection and an honest appraisal of your abilities and areas for improvement. This process isn't just about listing what you're good at or where you fall short; it's about understanding how these traits influence your behaviors, decisions, and ultimately, your success.

Consider your strengths first. These are the qualities, skills, and abilities that come naturally to you or have been honed through experience and effort. They are the aspects of yourself that you can rely on to perform well in various situations. Identifying your strengths requires introspection and feedback from others. Reflect on moments when you felt particularly effective or received praise. What qualities were you exhibiting? Perhaps you have a knack for problem-solving, a talent for communication, or an ability to stay calm under pressure. These attributes are your strengths.

Seeking feedback from trusted friends, family, or colleagues can provide insights you might overlook. They can offer perspectives on your behavior and performance in different contexts. Additionally, professional assessments like the StrengthsFinder or the Myers-Briggs Type Indicator can provide structured insights into your personality and abilities. These tools can highlight strengths you might not have fully recognized and suggest ways to leverage them.

However, simply knowing your strengths isn't enough. You need to understand how to use them effectively. This involves aligning your strengths with your goals. For instance, if one of your strengths is creativity, find ways to incorporate creative thinking into your work or personal projects. If you're a strong communicator, seek roles or activities that allow you to use this skill. By aligning your strengths with your objectives, you can maximize your potential and achieve more satisfying results.

While understanding your strengths is empowering, recognizing your weaknesses is equally important. Weaknesses are areas where you struggle or lack proficiency. Identifying them requires honesty and courage, as it can be uncomfortable to acknowledge your limitations. Start by reflecting on situations where you faced difficulties or underperformed. What were the contributing factors? Were there specific skills or knowledge you were lacking? Perhaps you struggle with time management, have difficulty with public speaking, or find it hard to stay organized.

Feedback from others can be invaluable here as well. Constructive criticism can highlight areas for improvement that you might not see yourself. Approach this feedback with an open mind and a willingness to learn. Remember, identifying weaknesses isn't about self-criticism; it's about recognizing opportunities for growth.

Once you've identified your weaknesses, the next step is to address them. This doesn't mean you need to turn every weakness into a strength. Instead, focus on mitigating the impact of your weaknesses and finding ways to improve in critical areas. For example, if time management is a challenge, you can adopt strategies like creating detailed schedules, setting priorities, and using productivity tools. If public speaking is a weakness, consider joining a group like Toastmasters to practice and build confidence.

Sometimes, the best approach to dealing with weaknesses is to delegate or seek support. If organization isn't your strong suit, using organizational tools or working with someone who excels in this area can help. By acknowledging your limitations and seeking assistance, you can focus more on your strengths and achieve better overall performance.

Balancing your strengths and weaknesses is key. Relying solely on your strengths can lead to complacency, while focusing only on your weaknesses can be discouraging. Strive for a balanced approach where you leverage your strengths to their fullest while continuously working on improving your weaknesses. This balanced approach fosters resilience and adaptability, essential traits for personal growth.

To gain a comprehensive understanding of your strengths and weaknesses, it's helpful to conduct a SWOT analysis. This strategic planning tool, commonly used in business, can be adapted for personal development. SWOT stands for Strengths, Weaknesses, Opportunities, and Threats. Strengths and weaknesses are internal factors, while opportunities and threats are external. By analyzing these four areas, you can develop a clearer picture of where you stand and how to move forward.

Start by listing your strengths and weaknesses as discussed earlier. Then, identify opportunities that can help you leverage your strengths or improve your weaknesses. These might include new learning opportunities, potential mentors, or changes in your environment that can support your growth. Conversely, identify threats that could hinder your progress, such as a lack of resources, unsupportive relationships, or negative habits.

Once you have a SWOT analysis, you can create an action plan. Set specific, measurable goals to capitalize on your strengths, take advantage of opportunities, and address your weaknesses and threats. This structured approach ensures that you are not just aware of your strengths and weaknesses but are actively working towards personal growth.

Incorporating regular self-assessment into your routine is essential for ongoing personal growth. Set aside time periodically to review your strengths and weaknesses. Reflect on your progress and adjust your strategies as needed. This continuous self-evaluation ensures that you remain aware of your development and can make timely adjustments to your plans.

Another effective method for identifying and developing your strengths and weaknesses is through setting and pursuing challenging goals. When you push yourself beyond your comfort zone, you not only test your limits but also discover new strengths and weaknesses. For instance, taking on a leadership role might reveal strengths in decision-making and weaknesses in delegation. These experiences provide valuable insights that can guide your personal development efforts.

It's also important to cultivate a growth mindset, a concept introduced by psychologist Carol Dweck. A growth mindset is the belief that abilities and intelligence can be developed through dedication and hard work. This perspective encourages continuous learning and resilience in the face of challenges. By adopting a growth mindset, you can view your weaknesses as areas for development rather than fixed limitations. This attitude fosters a proactive approach to personal growth.

Engaging in lifelong learning is another powerful way to address weaknesses and strengthen your abilities. Continuously seek out new knowledge and skills through formal education, workshops, reading, and practical experiences. The more you learn, the better equipped you are to handle various situations and the more opportunities you have to discover and develop your strengths.

Building a supportive network can also aid in identifying and developing your strengths and weaknesses. Surround yourself with people who encourage your growth, provide honest feedback, and offer different perspectives. Mentors, coaches, and supportive peers can provide guidance and accountability, helping you stay on track with your personal development goals.

Finally, practice self-compassion throughout this journey. Recognizing your weaknesses can be challenging, and it's easy to become self-critical. Treat yourself with kindness and understanding, acknowledging that everyone has areas for improvement. Celebrate your progress, no matter how small, and maintain a positive outlook on your personal growth journey.

Overcoming Limiting Beliefs

Limiting beliefs are those ingrained notions that hold you back and prevent you from reaching your full potential. They are often formed in childhood, shaped by experiences, societal influences, and the opinions of others. These beliefs create self-imposed barriers that can hinder personal and professional growth. Overcoming limiting beliefs requires a conscious effort to identify, challenge, and replace them with empowering thoughts.

Imagine a young girl named Emma who loved to draw. She spent hours creating vibrant images, losing herself in the world of colors and shapes. One day, a teacher remarked that her drawings were not good enough. This offhand comment planted a seed of doubt in Emma's mind. Over time, it grew into a limiting belief: "I am not good at art." As Emma grew older, she stopped drawing altogether, convinced she lacked talent. This is how limiting beliefs can take root and influence our actions.

To overcome limiting beliefs, the first step is to identify them. This requires self-awareness and introspection. Pay attention to the thoughts that surface when you face challenges or opportunities. Do you find yourself thinking, "I can't do this," or "I'm not smart enough"? These are clues to your limiting beliefs. Writing them down can help make them more tangible and easier to confront.

Once you have identified your limiting beliefs, challenge their validity. Ask yourself where these beliefs come from and if they are based on facts or assumptions. Emma, for instance, could revisit her teacher's comment and recognize that it was just one person's opinion, not an absolute truth. Questioning the origins and accuracy of your beliefs is a powerful way to weaken their hold on you.

Another effective strategy is to reframe your limiting beliefs into positive, empowering statements. This process, known as cognitive restructuring, involves replacing negative thoughts with constructive ones. For example, Emma could change "I am not good at art" to "I can improve my art skills with practice." This shift in perspective opens up possibilities for growth and encourages a proactive approach to overcoming limitations.

Visualization is a potent tool in this journey. Picture yourself succeeding and achieving your goals. Imagine the feelings of accomplishment and joy that come with it. This mental imagery can help reinforce positive beliefs and motivate you to take action. Athletes often use visualization to enhance their performance, and you can apply the same technique to overcome your limiting beliefs.

Surrounding yourself with supportive and encouraging people can also make a significant difference. Seek out friends, mentors, or coaches who believe in your potential and can offer constructive feedback. Their positive influence can help counteract the negative impact of limiting beliefs and provide you with the confidence to pursue your goals.

Emma decided to join an art class to reignite her passion for drawing. Initially, she felt nervous and doubted her abilities. However, the supportive environment and constructive feedback from her instructor helped her regain confidence. Over time, her skills improved, and she realized that her limiting belief was unfounded. By taking action and seeking support, Emma was able to overcome her self-doubt and rediscover her love for art.

Taking small, consistent steps towards your goals is crucial in overcoming limiting beliefs. Break down your objectives into manageable tasks and celebrate each milestone. This approach not only makes the process less overwhelming but also builds momentum and reinforces positive beliefs. As you achieve small successes, your confidence grows, making it easier to tackle bigger challenges.

Consider the story of Thomas Edison, who faced numerous failures before successfully inventing the electric light bulb. Each setback could have reinforced a limiting belief, but Edison viewed them as learning opportunities. His persistence and belief in his ability to succeed eventually led to one of the most significant inventions in history. Edison's story illustrates the importance of perseverance and maintaining a positive mindset despite obstacles.

Practicing self-compassion is essential in this journey. Recognize that everyone has limiting beliefs and that overcoming them is a process. Be kind to yourself when you encounter setbacks or negative thoughts. Instead of being self-critical, remind yourself that growth takes time and effort. Self-compassion fosters resilience and helps you stay motivated even when progress seems slow.

Journaling can be a valuable tool for reflecting on your progress and maintaining a positive mindset. Regularly write about your experiences, challenges, and achievements. This practice can help you track your growth, identify patterns in your thinking, and reinforce positive beliefs. Additionally, journaling provides a safe space to express your thoughts and emotions, which can be therapeutic and empowering.

Mindfulness and meditation are also effective techniques for overcoming limiting beliefs. These practices help you become more aware of your thoughts and emotions, allowing you to observe them without judgment. By cultivating mindfulness, you can create a mental space to challenge negative beliefs and replace them with empowering ones. Meditation, in particular, can reduce stress and increase self-awareness, making it easier to address limiting beliefs.

Consider adopting a growth mindset, a concept developed by psychologist Carol Dweck. A growth mindset is the belief that abilities and intelligence can be developed through effort and learning. Embracing this mindset encourages you to view challenges as opportunities for growth rather than threats. It shifts your focus from proving yourself to improving yourself, making it easier to overcome limiting beliefs.

Emma's journey to overcome her limiting belief about her artistic abilities was transformative. She not only regained her passion for drawing but also discovered new strengths and talents. Her experience highlights the power of challenging and changing limiting beliefs. By identifying, questioning, and reframing these beliefs, you can unlock your potential and achieve your goals.

Remember that overcoming limiting beliefs is not a one-time event but an ongoing process. New challenges and experiences may bring up old doubts or create new ones. Stay vigilant and continue to apply the strategies discussed in this chapter. With persistence and self-compassion, you can break free from the constraints of limiting beliefs and pursue a fulfilling and successful life.

In your journey, you may encounter moments of doubt or fear. These feelings are natural and part of the process. Use them as opportunities to reaffirm your positive beliefs and remind yourself of your progress. Each time you confront and overcome a limiting belief, you build resilience and confidence.

Setting Realistic and Achievable Goals

Setting realistic and achievable goals is a cornerstone of personal and professional development. Goals provide direction, motivation, and a benchmark for measuring progress. However, the key to effective goal-setting lies in ensuring that the goals are both attainable and meaningful. Without this balance, goals can become sources of frustration rather than motivation.

Consider James, a marketing professional who aspired to become a department head within a year. His ambition was commendable, but he had not considered the necessary steps and skills required to achieve such a leap. When the year ended without a promotion, James felt disheartened and doubted his capabilities. His experience underscores the importance of setting goals that are not only ambitious but also realistic.

The first step in setting realistic and achievable goals is to be specific. Vague goals like "I want to be successful" or "I want to get fit" lack the clarity needed to guide actions. Instead, specificity helps in creating a clear roadmap. For instance, if James had set a goal to "increase my sales by 20% in the next six months," he would have had a concrete target to work towards.

Specific goals provide a clear focus and make it easier to monitor progress.

Measurable goals are equally crucial. Being able to track progress allows you to stay motivated and adjust strategies if necessary. James could have set measurable milestones such as "attend three professional development workshops" or "complete a certification course in digital marketing." These milestones not only break the larger goal into manageable parts but also provide a sense of accomplishment as each one is achieved.

Achievability is another critical aspect. Goals should stretch your abilities but remain within the realm of possibility. Setting unattainable goals can lead to frustration and demotivation. James's goal of becoming a department head within a year might have been more realistic if he had aimed to first secure a team leader position. Achievable goals consider current skills, resources, and time constraints, ensuring that you are not setting yourself up for failure.

Relevance is also vital in goal-setting. Goals should align with your broader life objectives and values. If a goal does not resonate with your personal or professional aspirations, maintaining motivation can be challenging. For James, aiming for a leadership role in a department where he had no genuine interest would not have been fulfilling. Ensuring that your goals align with your passions and long-term visions enhances commitment and drive.

Time-bound goals add a sense of urgency and help prioritize tasks. A deadline creates a time frame within which you aim to achieve your goal, preventing procrastination. James could have set a time-bound goal such as "gain the necessary skills for a leadership role within two years." This timeline would have given him a clear end date and helped him pace his efforts.

The SMART criteria—Specific, Measurable, Achievable, Relevant, and Time-bound—provide a comprehensive framework for setting effective goals. By adhering to these principles, you can create well-defined and attainable objectives.

Visualization is a powerful technique in goal-setting. Imagining yourself achieving your goals can enhance motivation and clarify the steps needed to get there. James could have visualized himself leading a team, managing projects, and receiving accolades for his performance. This mental imagery can make the goal feel more tangible and inspire the necessary actions to achieve it.

Breaking down goals into smaller, actionable steps is essential. Large goals can be overwhelming, but dividing them into smaller tasks makes them more manageable. James's goal of becoming a department head could be broken down into steps such as "develop leadership skills," "network with industry professionals," and "gain experience in team management." Each step would bring him closer to his ultimate goal while making the process less daunting.

Accountability plays a significant role in achieving goals. Sharing your goals with a mentor, friend, or colleague can provide external motivation and support. James could have discussed his aspirations with a mentor who could offer guidance and hold him accountable. Regular check-ins with an accountability partner can help maintain focus and commitment.

Flexibility is also important. Life is unpredictable, and circumstances can change. Being adaptable and willing to revise your goals as needed ensures that they remain realistic and achievable. If James encountered unexpected challenges, he could reassess his timeline or adjust his milestones without abandoning his ultimate goal.

Celebrating small victories along the way is crucial for maintaining motivation. Acknowledging progress, no matter how minor, reinforces positive behavior and boosts morale. James could celebrate milestones such as completing a training program or successfully leading a project. These celebrations provide a sense of accomplishment and encourage continued effort.

Reflecting on past successes and failures can provide valuable insights for future goal-setting. Understanding what worked and what didn't helps refine your approach. James could analyze past projects to identify skills he excelled at and areas needing improvement. This reflection can guide the setting of more effective and realistic goals.

Self-discipline and time management are fundamental to achieving goals. Prioritizing tasks, avoiding procrastination, and maintaining focus are essential. James could create a daily schedule allocating specific time slots for skill development, networking, and project management. Consistent effort and disciplined time management ensure steady progress towards the goal.

Seeking feedback is another valuable practice in goal-setting. Constructive criticism from peers, mentors, or supervisors can provide new perspectives and highlight areas for improvement. James could regularly seek feedback on his leadership skills, allowing him to make necessary adjustments and improve continuously.

Finally, maintaining a positive mindset is crucial. Self-belief and optimism can drive perseverance even in the face of challenges. James should remind himself of his strengths and past achievements to stay motivated. A positive mindset fosters resilience and encourages a proactive approach to overcoming obstacles.

James's journey towards becoming a department head, though initially challenging, became manageable through realistic and achievable goal-setting. By being specific, measurable, achievable, relevant, and time-bound, he created a clear path towards his objective. Visualization, breaking down goals, accountability, flexibility, celebrating small victories, reflection, self-discipline, seeking feedback, and maintaining a positive mindset were all integral to his success.

The Role of Self-awareness

Self-awareness is a crucial element in personal growth and professional success. It involves a deep understanding of one's own emotions, strengths, weaknesses, values, and motivations. This introspective skill is foundational for effective decision-making, forming healthy relationships, and achieving long-term goals. The journey toward self-awareness is deeply personal, yet it universally affects how we navigate the world around us.

Consider the story of Sarah, a young professional who excelled in her role as a project manager. Despite her success, Sarah often felt overwhelmed and dissatisfied. She struggled with understanding why she felt this way, given her accomplishments. Through the process of developing self-awareness, Sarah discovered that her dissatisfaction stemmed from a misalignment between her values and her daily tasks. Her true passion lay in creative problem-solving, yet her role had become predominantly administrative. This realization was the first step in her journey toward greater fulfillment and effectiveness at work.

Self-awareness begins with introspection. Taking time to reflect on your thoughts, feelings, and behaviors is essential. This can be achieved through journaling, meditation, or simply setting aside quiet moments in your day to consider your experiences. By regularly engaging in introspection, you start to notice patterns in how you react to various situations, what triggers stress or joy, and how your interactions with others unfold.

Another critical aspect of self-awareness is understanding your strengths and weaknesses. Knowing what you excel at allows you to leverage your skills effectively, while acknowledging areas for improvement enables you to seek development opportunities. For Sarah, recognizing her strength in creative thinking and her weakness in administrative tasks helped her restructure her role to better align with her talents. She began delegating administrative duties and focusing more on innovative projects, leading to increased job satisfaction and productivity.

Emotional intelligence is closely linked to self-awareness. It involves recognizing and managing your own emotions as well as understanding and influencing the emotions of others. High emotional intelligence enhances communication, conflict resolution, and leadership abilities. Sarah's journey highlighted the importance of emotional intelligence. By becoming more attuned to her emotions, she learned to manage stress and communicate more effectively with her team. This not only improved her own well-being but also fostered a more collaborative and positive work environment.

Feedback from others is a valuable tool for developing self-awareness. Constructive feedback provides external perspectives that you might not have considered. Sarah sought feedback from her colleagues and mentors, which revealed blind spots in her self-perception. For instance, while she saw herself as approachable, some team members perceived her as distant due to her focus on tasks. This insight allowed her to adjust her behavior to become more engaged and supportive.

Mindfulness practices can significantly enhance self-awareness. Mindfulness involves being fully present in the moment, observing your thoughts and feelings without judgment. This practice helps reduce stress, improve focus, and increase emotional regulation. Sarah incorporated mindfulness techniques into her daily routine, such as mindful breathing and body scans. These practices helped her stay grounded, recognize her emotional states, and respond to challenges with greater clarity and composure.

Understanding your values is another essential component of self-awareness. Your values guide your decisions and actions, shaping your personal and professional life. When your actions align with your values, you experience greater fulfillment and integrity. Sarah's introspection revealed that creativity and innovation were core values for her. This realization prompted her to seek roles and projects that allowed her to express these values, leading to a more meaningful and satisfying career.

Self-awareness also involves recognizing your impact on others. Your behavior and attitude can influence the dynamics of your team, family, and social circles. Being aware of this impact allows you to foster positive relationships and create a supportive environment. Sarah realized that her stress and dissatisfaction were affecting her team's morale. By addressing her own issues and becoming more mindful of her interactions, she was able to lead with empathy and support, enhancing the overall team dynamic.

Personal growth and self-awareness are intertwined. The more you understand yourself, the better equipped you are to pursue personal development. This might involve seeking new learning opportunities, setting personal and professional goals, or engaging in activities that challenge and expand your capabilities. Sarah committed to continuous learning by attending workshops and reading extensively on creativity and leadership. This commitment to growth not only enriched her skills but also reinforced her self-awareness journey.

Self-awareness is not a one-time achievement but an ongoing process. It requires regular reflection, feedback, and adjustment. Life experiences, both positive and negative, contribute to this continuous journey. Sarah faced setbacks and successes, each providing valuable lessons and deeper insights into her own character and aspirations. Embracing this iterative process allowed her to remain adaptable and resilient in the face of challenges.

Building self-awareness can sometimes be uncomfortable, as it involves confronting aspects of yourself that you might prefer to ignore. However, this discomfort is a necessary part of growth. By facing and understanding these aspects, you can make conscious choices to improve and evolve. Sarah experienced discomfort when she realized how her behavior was perceived by others. Yet, this realization was crucial for her development as a leader and a person.

The role of self-awareness extends beyond individual benefits; it influences your interactions and contributions to the broader community. A self-aware individual is more likely to act with empathy, integrity, and social responsibility. Sarah's enhanced self-awareness enabled her to lead her team with greater compassion and understanding, fostering a supportive and productive work environment. This positive impact extended beyond her immediate team, contributing to a more positive organizational culture.

Chapter 3

Building a Growth Mindset

What is a Growth Mindset

A growth mindset is a transformative way of thinking that emphasizes the potential for development and improvement over time. Unlike a fixed mindset, which views abilities as static and unchangeable, a growth mindset believes that skills and intelligence can be honed through dedication and hard work. This concept, popularized by psychologist Carol Dweck, has profound implications for personal and professional development.

Imagine a student named Alex who struggles with mathematics. With a fixed mindset, Alex might think, "I'm just not good at math," and avoid challenging problems. This mindset limits Alex's potential, as he believes his abilities are innate and unchangeable. On the other hand, if Alex adopts a growth mindset, he would approach math with the belief that effort and persistence can lead to improvement. This shift in perspective encourages Alex to embrace challenges, learn from mistakes, and ultimately enhance his skills.

The foundation of a growth mindset is the belief that abilities can be developed. This outlook fosters resilience and a willingness to take on challenges. When faced with a difficult task, individuals with a growth mindset are more likely to see it as an opportunity to learn rather than a threat to their self-esteem. This mindset not only enhances learning and performance but also builds confidence and perseverance.

One of the key components of a growth mindset is the understanding that effort is essential for success. In a fixed mindset, effort is often seen as a sign of weakness—if you have to try hard, you must not be naturally talented. However, a growth mindset reframes effort as a necessary part of the learning process. This perspective encourages individuals to put in the time and energy needed to master new skills and overcome obstacles.

Consider the story of Thomas Edison, who famously failed thousands of times before successfully inventing the light bulb. Edison's perseverance exemplifies a growth mindset. He viewed each failure as a step toward eventual success, rather than a reflection of his capabilities. This relentless pursuit of improvement, driven by a growth mindset, ultimately led to one of the most significant inventions in history.

Another crucial aspect of a growth mindset is the ability to learn from criticism. In a fixed mindset, criticism is often perceived as a personal attack, leading to defensiveness and avoidance. Conversely, a growth mindset views constructive feedback as valuable information that can guide improvement. By embracing feedback, individuals with a growth mindset can identify areas for growth and make necessary adjustments to their approach.

The story of Oprah Winfrey illustrates the power of learning from criticism. Early in her career, Winfrey faced significant setbacks, including being fired from her first television job. Instead of allowing this failure to define her, she used the feedback to refine her skills and ultimately became one of the most influential media personalities in the world. Her success is a testament to the resilience and adaptability fostered by a growth mindset.

A growth mindset also promotes the idea that setbacks and failures are part of the learning process. Rather than fearing failure, individuals with a growth mindset understand that it provides valuable lessons and opportunities for growth. This perspective reduces the fear of making mistakes and encourages a more adventurous and innovative approach to challenges.

Take J.K. Rowling, for example. Before achieving fame with the Harry Potter series, Rowling faced numerous rejections from publishers. Her perseverance and willingness to learn from each rejection exemplify a growth mindset. Instead of giving up, she continued to refine her manuscript, eventually creating one of the most beloved literary series of all time.

Cultivating a growth mindset involves several practical steps. One effective strategy is to reframe challenges as opportunities. When faced with a difficult task, consciously shift your perspective to see it as a chance to learn and grow. This simple change in mindset can have a profound impact on your motivation and resilience.

Another strategy is to focus on the process rather than the outcome. Instead of fixating on the end result, pay attention to the steps you are taking and the progress you are making. This approach helps to reduce anxiety about performance and fosters a greater appreciation for the learning journey. By valuing the process, you can maintain motivation even when progress is slow or setbacks occur.

Seeking out challenges is also important for developing a growth mindset. Actively pursue tasks that stretch your abilities and push you out of your comfort zone. These experiences provide valuable opportunities for growth and help to build the resilience needed to tackle future challenges. Embracing challenges with a growth mindset transforms them from daunting obstacles into exciting opportunities for development.

Additionally, it is essential to cultivate a positive attitude towards mistakes. View errors as learning experiences rather than failures. When you make a mistake, take the time to analyze what went wrong and how you can improve. This reflective practice turns setbacks into valuable learning moments and reinforces the belief that abilities can be developed through effort and perseverance.

Surrounding yourself with a supportive and growth-oriented community can also enhance your mindset. Engage with individuals who encourage your efforts and provide constructive feedback. A positive and collaborative environment fosters a culture of continuous improvement and reinforces the principles of a growth mindset.

The story of Michael Jordan, widely regarded as one of the greatest basketball players of all time, underscores the importance of a growth-oriented community. Jordan was famously cut from his high school basketball team, but he used this setback as motivation to improve. With the support of his coaches and teammates, he honed his skills through relentless practice and perseverance, ultimately achieving unparalleled success in his sport.

Parents, educators, and leaders play a crucial role in fostering a growth mindset in others. By praising effort rather than innate ability, they can encourage a focus on learning and improvement. Providing constructive feedback and celebrating progress reinforces the belief that abilities can be developed. Creating an environment that values persistence and resilience helps to instill a growth mindset in those around you.

Carol Dweck's research has shown that the language we use can significantly impact mindset. Phrases like "You worked really hard on this" or "I can see you put a lot of effort into this project" emphasize the importance of effort and improvement. This type of praise encourages a growth mindset by highlighting the value of persistence and hard work.

The benefits of a growth mindset extend beyond individual development. In professional settings, organizations that cultivate a growth mindset culture see increased innovation, collaboration, and adaptability. Employees feel more empowered to take risks, share ideas, and learn from failures. This collective growth mindset drives organizational success and fosters a more dynamic and resilient workforce.

Techniques to Develop a Growth Mindset

Developing a growth mindset is like planting a seed in fertile soil and nurturing it to full bloom. This mindset, which emphasizes the potential for development and improvement, can be cultivated through deliberate practice and specific techniques. Here's how you can foster a growth mindset and unlock your full potential.

First, embrace the power of "yet." When you encounter a challenging task, instead of thinking, "I can't do this," add the word "yet" to the end of the sentence. This small linguistic shift can make a significant difference in your outlook. For instance, saying "I can't solve this problem yet" suggests that with effort and time, you will be able to overcome the challenge. This approach encourages you to see obstacles as temporary and surmountable, rather than permanent roadblocks.

Another effective technique is to set learning goals instead of performance goals. Performance goals focus on the outcome, such as getting an A on a test or winning a competition. Learning goals, on the other hand, emphasize the process and the improvement, like understanding a new concept or mastering a skill. By focusing on learning goals, you shift your attention to the journey of growth and development, which is more aligned with a growth mindset.

Consider the journey of Serena Williams, one of the greatest tennis players of all time. Early in her career, Serena faced numerous setbacks, including injuries and losses. However, she consistently set learning goals for herself, such as improving her serve or enhancing her footwork. This focus on continuous improvement helped her to become not only a champion but also an enduring icon in the sport.

Reflecting on your progress regularly can also reinforce a growth mindset. Keep a journal where you document your efforts, challenges, and improvements. This practice allows you to see how far you've come and recognize the value of persistence. By reviewing your journey, you can identify patterns, learn from your experiences, and celebrate small victories along the way. This reflection helps to solidify the belief that growth is possible and that effort leads to improvement.

Additionally, reframe failures as opportunities for learning. When you experience a setback, instead of viewing it as a failure, ask yourself, "What can I learn from this?" This perspective encourages you to see mistakes as valuable feedback rather than as a reflection of your abilities. Analyzing what went wrong and how you can improve helps to build resilience and fosters a more positive attitude towards challenges.

Consider the story of Steve Jobs, the co-founder of Apple. After being ousted from the company he helped create, Jobs could have viewed this setback as a personal failure. Instead, he used the experience to learn and grow, eventually returning to Apple and leading the company to unprecedented success. His ability to reframe failure as a learning opportunity was a key factor in his resilience and innovation.

Surrounding yourself with a growth-oriented community can also enhance your mindset. Engage with people who encourage your efforts, provide constructive feedback, and celebrate your progress. Being part of a supportive environment fosters a culture of continuous improvement and reinforces the principles of a growth mindset. This community can include mentors, peers, and even online groups that share your commitment to growth and development.

Visualization is another powerful tool for developing a growth mindset. Take a few moments each day to visualize yourself overcoming challenges, learning from mistakes, and achieving your goals. This mental rehearsal prepares your brain for real-life situations and strengthens your belief in your ability to grow. Visualization helps to build confidence and resilience, making it easier to tackle difficult tasks and persist in the face of setbacks.

Practicing mindfulness can also support the development of a growth mindset. Mindfulness involves being present in the moment and observing your thoughts and feelings without judgment. This practice helps you to become more aware of negative self-talk and fixed mindset beliefs. By acknowledging these thoughts and gently redirecting them towards a growth-oriented perspective, you can cultivate a more positive and resilient mindset.

The story of Michael Phelps, the most decorated Olympian of all time, illustrates the power of visualization and mindfulness. Phelps used visualization techniques to mentally rehearse his races, imagining every detail from start to finish. He also practiced mindfulness to stay focused and calm under pressure. These techniques contributed to his extraordinary success and his ability to maintain a growth mindset throughout his career.

Another practical strategy is to seek out and embrace feedback. Constructive criticism provides valuable insights into areas where you can improve. Instead of viewing feedback as a negative judgment, see it as an opportunity to learn and grow. Actively seek feedback from mentors, peers, and supervisors, and use it to guide your efforts towards continuous improvement.

To cultivate a growth mindset in others, especially in children or team members, it's important to praise effort rather than innate ability. Statements like "You worked really hard on this" or "I can see you put a lot of effort into this project" emphasize the importance of effort and persistence. This type of praise encourages a focus on the process of learning and reinforces the belief that abilities can be developed through hard work.

Creating a culture of curiosity also promotes a growth mindset. Encourage yourself and others to ask questions, explore new ideas, and seek out new experiences. Curiosity drives the pursuit of knowledge and fosters a love of learning. When you approach life with a sense of wonder and a desire to understand, you naturally adopt a growth-oriented perspective.

The journey of Elon Musk, the entrepreneur behind companies like Tesla and SpaceX, highlights the importance of curiosity. Musk's relentless curiosity and desire to solve complex problems have driven his innovations and successes. His willingness to explore new fields and learn from failures exemplifies a growth mindset in action.

Lastly, practice self-compassion. Be kind to yourself when you encounter difficulties or make mistakes. Recognize that struggle and setbacks are part of the learning process. Treat yourself with the same understanding and encouragement that you would offer to a friend. Self-compassion helps to maintain motivation and resilience, making it easier to persist in the face of challenges.

Embracing Challenges and Learning from Failure

Stepping into the unknown often feels daunting, yet it is through embracing challenges and learning from failure that we find our greatest growth. When you shift your perspective to see obstacles as opportunities, you open the door to endless possibilities. This mindset is crucial for personal and professional development, and it begins with a willingness to face difficulties head-on.

Consider the story of Thomas Edison, one of the most prolific inventors in history. Edison's journey to invent the light bulb was riddled with failures—over a thousand unsuccessful attempts, to be precise. When asked about these failures, Edison famously replied, "I have not failed. I've just found 10,000 ways that won't work." This perspective highlights the essence of embracing challenges: seeing each setback not as a defeat but as a stepping stone to success.

To effectively embrace challenges, start by setting clear and attainable goals. Break down larger objectives into smaller, manageable tasks. This approach not only makes daunting projects feel more achievable but also provides frequent opportunities for success and learning. When you accomplish these smaller tasks, you build momentum and confidence, making it easier to tackle the next challenge.

Take, for example, the journey of learning a new language. If you set a goal to become fluent in Spanish within a year, the task might seem overwhelming. However, by breaking it down into smaller goals—such as learning basic vocabulary, practicing simple conversations, and gradually advancing to more complex grammar—you create a structured path that makes the larger goal attainable. Each milestone reached provides motivation and a sense of accomplishment.

Another strategy to embrace challenges is to cultivate a mindset of curiosity. Approach each new problem with a sense of wonder and a desire to learn. Instead of seeing challenges as threats, view them as puzzles waiting to be solved. This shift in mindset can transform anxiety into excitement and drive you to explore new solutions and ideas.

Consider the case of Marie Curie, the pioneering scientist who conducted groundbreaking research on radioactivity. Despite facing significant obstacles, including limited resources and societal biases, Curie's insatiable curiosity drove her to persevere. Her dedication to understanding the unknown led to monumental discoveries that revolutionized science and medicine. Curie's story exemplifies how a curious mindset can fuel resilience and innovation.

To learn from failure, it's essential to reframe your understanding of what failure means. Instead of viewing it as a negative outcome, see it as feedback. Each failure provides valuable data on what doesn't work, which can be used to refine your approach and improve your strategies. This perspective turns failures into opportunities for growth and learning.

Reflecting on your failures is a key part of this process. When you experience a setback, take time to analyze what happened. Ask yourself questions like: What went wrong? What could I have done differently? What have I learned from this experience? By dissecting your failures, you gain insights that can help you avoid similar mistakes in the future and enhance your problem-solving skills.

The story of J.K. Rowling, author of the Harry Potter series, offers a compelling example of learning from failure. Before achieving literary success, Rowling faced numerous rejections from publishers. Instead of giving up, she used the feedback from these rejections to refine her manuscript and improve her storytelling. Her persistence and willingness to learn from failure eventually led to one of the most successful book series in history.

Another practical approach to embracing challenges is to seek out new and uncomfortable experiences. Stepping outside your comfort zone regularly can help you build resilience and adaptability. When you expose yourself to new challenges, you develop the skills and confidence needed to handle unexpected situations and complex problems.

Consider the practice of public speaking. For many, speaking in front of an audience is a significant challenge. However, by intentionally seeking out opportunities to practice public speaking—whether through joining a local Toastmasters club, giving presentations at work, or even speaking up in meetings—you gradually become more comfortable and skilled. Each experience, regardless of how it goes, contributes to your growth and ability to handle similar challenges in the future.

Embracing challenges also involves surrounding yourself with a supportive community. Engage with people who encourage your efforts, provide constructive feedback, and celebrate your progress. A strong support network can offer motivation and different perspectives, helping you navigate difficulties more effectively. This community can be made up of mentors, peers, family, or friends who share your commitment to growth.

The story of Malala Yousafzai, the young activist for girls' education, illustrates the power of a supportive community. Despite facing life-threatening challenges, Malala continued her advocacy work, supported by her family and global community. Their encouragement and belief in her mission enabled Malala to persevere and amplify her message on an international stage.

Developing resilience is another crucial aspect of embracing challenges. Resilience allows you to bounce back from setbacks and maintain your focus on long-term goals. One way to build resilience is through practicing self-care and maintaining a healthy work-life balance. Taking care of your physical and mental well-being ensures that you have the energy and clarity needed to tackle challenges effectively.

Athletes often exemplify resilience through their training and recovery routines. Consider the story of Michael Jordan, widely regarded as one of the greatest basketball players of all time. Jordan faced numerous setbacks, including being cut from his high school basketball team and enduring multiple injuries throughout his career. His resilience, fueled by rigorous training, self-care, and an unwavering commitment to his goals, enabled him to achieve unparalleled success.

To foster a growth-oriented approach, practice gratitude and positive thinking. Focus on the progress you've made and the lessons you've learned, rather than dwelling on setbacks. Celebrating small victories can boost morale and reinforce the belief that you are capable of overcoming challenges.

The journey of Oprah Winfrey, a media mogul and philanthropist, exemplifies the power of positive thinking and gratitude. Despite a challenging upbringing and numerous professional setbacks, Winfrey maintained a positive outlook and focused on her long-term vision. Her gratitude for each step of her journey, combined with a relentless pursuit of her goals, led to her becoming one of the most influential figures in media and beyond.

Finally, remember that embracing challenges and learning from failure is an ongoing process. It requires continuous effort, reflection, and adaptation. By consistently applying these principles, you can develop the resilience and mindset needed to navigate life's complexities and achieve your fullest potential.

The Power of Positive Thinking

Positive thinking transforms not only how you perceive the world but also how you interact with it. Harnessing this power can lead to profound changes in your personal and professional life, enabling you to navigate challenges with resilience and grace. Unlike fleeting moments of optimism, positive thinking is a sustained attitude that influences your actions and decisions, creating a ripple effect that enhances your overall well-being.

Imagine starting your day with a simple affirmation: "Today is going to be a good day." This small, intentional act sets the tone for your day, preparing your mind to seek out and appreciate positive experiences. It's not about ignoring difficulties but about choosing to focus on what's good. By shifting your mindset, you unlock the ability to manage stress more effectively and build stronger relationships.

Consider the story of Viktor Frankl, an Austrian neurologist, psychiatrist, and Holocaust survivor. During his time in concentration camps, Frankl observed that those who maintained a hopeful and positive outlook were more likely to endure the harsh conditions. His experiences led to the development of logotherapy, a form of existential analysis that emphasizes finding meaning in life. Frankl's work underscores the profound impact that positive thinking can have, even in the most dire circumstances.

To cultivate positive thinking, start by practicing gratitude. Each day, take a moment to reflect on what you are thankful for. This practice can be as simple as jotting down three things that went well or expressing appreciation to someone who made a difference in your day. Gratitude shifts your focus from what's lacking to what's abundant, fostering a sense of contentment and joy.

Another effective strategy is to reframe negative thoughts. When faced with a challenging situation, ask yourself how you can view it from a more positive perspective. For instance, instead of thinking, "I can't do this," try, "This is an opportunity to learn and grow." This subtle change in wording can significantly alter your emotional response and motivate you to take constructive action.

Mindfulness and meditation are also powerful tools for nurturing a positive mindset. These practices help you become more aware of your thoughts and feelings, allowing you to respond rather than react to situations. By cultivating a state of present-moment awareness, you can reduce stress, increase emotional regulation, and enhance your overall sense of well-being.

The story of Jon Kabat-Zinn, the founder of Mindfulness-Based Stress Reduction (MBSR), illustrates the impact of mindfulness on positive thinking. Kabat-Zinn's program has helped countless individuals manage chronic pain, reduce anxiety, and improve their quality of life. His work highlights the connection between mindfulness, positive thinking, and overall health.

Surrounding yourself with positive influences is another crucial aspect of fostering a positive mindset. Engage with people who uplift and inspire you, and seek out environments that support your growth. This might involve joining groups with shared interests, participating in community activities, or simply spending more time with loved ones who encourage and support you.

Think of the story of Helen Keller, who, despite losing her sight and hearing at a young age, went on to become an influential author, lecturer, and advocate. Keller's remarkable achievements were made possible in part by the unwavering support of her teacher, Anne Sullivan. This relationship exemplifies how positive influences can empower individuals to overcome significant challenges and achieve greatness.

To maintain a positive outlook, it's also important to take care of your physical health. Regular exercise, a balanced diet, and adequate sleep all contribute to a healthy mind and body, creating a foundation for positive thinking. Physical activity, in particular, has been shown to boost mood and reduce symptoms of anxiety and depression. Even a simple walk in nature can have a profound effect on your mental state.

Consider the case of Haruki Murakami, the acclaimed novelist who credits his physical fitness routine with enhancing his creativity and mental clarity. Murakami's commitment to running and other forms of exercise has not only improved his physical health but also contributed to his enduring success as a writer. His story demonstrates the interconnectedness of physical well-being and positive thinking.

Setting realistic goals and celebrating small achievements can also reinforce a positive mindset. Break down your larger objectives into manageable steps, and acknowledge your progress along the way. This approach provides a sense of accomplishment and keeps you motivated, even when the ultimate goal seems distant.

The journey of Jane Goodall, the renowned primatologist, serves as a powerful example. Goodall's groundbreaking research on chimpanzees began with small, incremental observations that eventually led to significant scientific discoveries. Her dedication and ability to celebrate each small step forward illustrate how a positive and methodical approach can lead to extraordinary outcomes.

Another way to enhance positive thinking is to engage in activities that bring you joy and fulfillment. Whether it's a hobby, volunteering, or spending time with loved ones, these activities can provide a sense of purpose and happiness. Doing what you love not only boosts your mood but also reinforces a positive outlook on life.

The story of Fred Rogers, the beloved television personality, highlights the importance of finding joy in your work. Rogers' genuine love for educating and nurturing children through his show, "Mister Rogers' Neighborhood," created a lasting impact on generations. His unwavering positivity and dedication to his passion serve as a testament to the power of finding fulfillment in what you do.

Lastly, it's essential to practice self-compassion. Treat yourself with the same kindness and understanding that you would offer to a friend. Acknowledge your efforts, forgive your mistakes, and recognize that setbacks are a natural part of life. Self-compassion fosters resilience and helps you maintain a positive outlook, even in the face of adversity.

The work of Dr. Kristin Neff, a leading researcher on self-compassion, demonstrates its profound benefits. Neff's studies have shown that self-compassionate individuals tend to experience greater emotional well-being, reduced stress, and increased resilience. Her research underscores the importance of being gentle with yourself as you navigate life's challenges.

Cultivating Resilience

Resilience is the remarkable ability to bounce back from adversity, to recover from setbacks, and to adapt to change. It is a crucial skill that can be developed and strengthened over time, enabling you to navigate life's challenges with greater ease and confidence. Cultivating resilience involves a combination of mindset, behaviors, and support systems that work together to bolster your capacity to cope with difficulties.

One of the foundational elements of resilience is maintaining a positive outlook. This doesn't mean ignoring problems or pretending everything is fine when it's not. Instead, it involves recognizing the difficulties while also believing in your ability to find solutions and overcome them. This mindset can be nurtured through practices such as gratitude and positive self-talk. By consistently focusing on what you are thankful for, you can shift your perspective from what is lacking to what is abundant in your life. Positive self-talk, on the other hand, involves replacing negative, self-defeating thoughts with affirmations that reinforce your strengths and capabilities.

Take the story of Nelson Mandela, who spent 27 years in prison under apartheid before becoming the president of South Africa. Mandela's resilience was rooted in his unwavering belief in justice and equality, coupled with his ability to maintain hope and optimism despite his circumstances. His story exemplifies how a positive outlook, even in the face of extreme adversity, can sustain resilience and lead to profound personal and societal change.

Another crucial component of resilience is the ability to manage stress effectively. Stress is an inevitable part of life, and how you respond to it can significantly impact your resilience. Developing healthy coping mechanisms, such as exercise, meditation, and hobbies, can help you manage stress more effectively. Regular physical activity, for example, has been shown to reduce stress hormones and trigger the release of endorphins, which are natural mood lifters. Similarly, mindfulness and meditation practices can help calm the mind, reduce anxiety, and enhance emotional regulation.

Consider the example of Serena Williams, one of the greatest tennis players of all time. Williams has faced numerous challenges throughout her career, including injuries, personal losses, and public scrutiny. Her resilience is partly attributed to her rigorous training regimen, which includes not only physical workouts but also mental conditioning through mindfulness and visualization techniques. By managing stress and maintaining mental clarity, Williams has been able to perform at the highest levels even under immense pressure.

Building strong relationships and seeking social support are also vital for resilience. Human beings are inherently social creatures, and having a network of supportive friends, family, and colleagues can provide a buffer against stress and adversity. These relationships offer emotional support, practical assistance, and a sense of belonging, all of which can enhance your ability to cope with challenges. It's important to nurture these connections by being present, listening actively, and offering support in return.

The story of Malala Yousafzai, the Pakistani activist for female education and the youngest Nobel Prize laureate, illustrates the power of social support in cultivating resilience. After surviving a gunshot wound to the head by the Taliban, Malala received an outpouring of support from around the world. This support, along with her family's encouragement, played a crucial role in her recovery and continued advocacy work. Malala's resilience is a testament to the strength that can be drawn from a supportive community.

Another key aspect of resilience is maintaining a sense of purpose and direction. Having clear goals and a sense of meaning in your life can provide motivation and a framework for making decisions, even in the face of setbacks. This sense of purpose can be derived from various sources, such as personal values, career aspirations, or a commitment to helping others. By aligning your actions with your deeper sense of purpose, you can navigate challenges with greater determination and clarity.

Victor Hugo, the French poet, novelist, and dramatist, found his sense of purpose through his literary work, which often addressed social injustices and human rights. Despite facing political exile and personal tragedies, Hugo's commitment to his ideals and his literary pursuits provided him with the resilience to continue his work. His legacy continues to inspire and impact society long after his time.

Flexibility and adaptability are also essential components of resilience. Life is unpredictable, and the ability to adjust your plans and expectations in response to changing circumstances is crucial for bouncing back from setbacks. This might involve developing new skills, seeking alternative solutions, or simply being open to change. By embracing flexibility, you can approach challenges as opportunities for growth rather than insurmountable obstacles.

The story of J.K. Rowling, the author of the Harry Potter series, serves as an inspiring example of adaptability. Before achieving literary success, Rowling faced numerous rejections from publishers and struggled with financial difficulties. Her resilience was demonstrated by her willingness to adapt and persevere, ultimately leading to the creation of one of the most beloved book series of all time. Rowling's journey highlights the importance of staying flexible and persistent in the pursuit of one's goals.

Resilience also involves the ability to learn from experiences, both positive and negative. Reflecting on past challenges and identifying the lessons learned can enhance your ability to handle future difficulties. This process of reflection helps you develop a deeper understanding of your strengths and areas for improvement, making you better equipped to tackle new challenges. Keeping a journal or discussing your experiences with a trusted mentor or friend can facilitate this reflective process.

The life of Thomas Edison, the prolific inventor, exemplifies the importance of learning from failure. Edison's numerous experiments often ended in failure, but he viewed each setback as a learning opportunity. His famous quote, "I have not failed. I've just found 10,000 ways that won't work," encapsulates his resilient mindset. Edison's ability to learn from his experiences ultimately led to groundbreaking inventions that have shaped modern life.

Chapter 4
Emotional Intelligence and Well-being

Understanding Emotional Intelligence

Emotional intelligence (EI) is the ability to identify, understand, manage, and harness one's own emotions and the emotions of others. Unlike intellectual intelligence (IQ), which is often measured by standardized tests and is relatively static, emotional intelligence can be developed and improved over time. It plays a crucial role in both personal and professional success, influencing how we make decisions, manage stress, and communicate with others.

Emotional intelligence begins with self-awareness, which is the ability to recognize and understand your own emotions. Self-awareness involves being conscious of your emotional state and how it affects your thoughts and behavior. It requires a deep and honest look at your emotional triggers, strengths, and weaknesses. By being aware of your emotions, you can better control your reactions and make more informed decisions.

Consider the example of Susan, a project manager who often felt overwhelmed by the demands of her job. Through self-awareness, she realized that her stress was primarily due to her perfectionism and fear of failure. By acknowledging these underlying emotions, Susan was able to address them more effectively, seeking support when needed and setting more realistic expectations for herself. This self-awareness not only improved her emotional well-being but also enhanced her performance at work.

The next component of emotional intelligence is self-regulation, which is the ability to manage and control your emotions, especially in stressful situations. Self-regulation involves staying calm under pressure, avoiding impulsive actions, and being adaptable to change. It requires practice and mindfulness, allowing you to respond to situations thoughtfully rather than reacting impulsively.

Think of a leader in a high-stakes environment, such as a surgeon in the operating room. The ability to remain composed and make clear, rational decisions under stress is critical. This self-regulation is not an innate talent but a skill developed through experience and conscious effort. By practicing self-regulation, you can improve your ability to handle challenges and maintain a positive outlook, even when faced with adversity.

Another key aspect of emotional intelligence is motivation. This goes beyond external rewards such as money or status, focusing instead on intrinsic motivation—the inner drive to pursue goals with energy and persistence. Emotionally intelligent individuals are often highly motivated, not just by personal gain but by a deeper sense of purpose and fulfillment.

Consider an entrepreneur like Elon Musk, whose motivation extends beyond financial success to a vision of advancing technology and exploring space. His intrinsic motivation fuels his resilience and innovation, driving him to overcome obstacles and push the boundaries of what is possible. By finding and nurturing your own intrinsic motivation, you can sustain your efforts and stay focused on your long-term goals.

Empathy, the ability to understand and share the feelings of others, is another crucial component of emotional intelligence. Empathy allows you to connect with others on a deeper level, fostering trust and understanding. It involves active listening, being attuned to nonverbal cues, and showing genuine concern for others' well-being.

Imagine a teacher who notices that a usually engaged student has become withdrawn and quiet. By showing empathy and taking the time to understand the student's situation, the teacher can offer support and create a safe, supportive environment. This empathetic approach not only helps the student but also strengthens the teacher-student relationship, promoting a more positive and effective learning experience.

Social skills, the final component of emotional intelligence, encompass a broad range of abilities that facilitate effective communication and relationship-building. These skills include conflict resolution, teamwork, leadership, and the ability to inspire and influence others. Good social skills are essential in both personal and professional settings, enabling you to navigate social complexities and build strong, positive relationships.

Consider the example of a team leader who excels in bringing people together, resolving conflicts, and fostering a collaborative environment. By leveraging their social skills, this leader can enhance team performance and morale, creating a more productive and harmonious workplace. Developing strong social skills involves continuous learning and practice, as well as a genuine interest in connecting with and understanding others.

Emotional intelligence is not a static trait but a dynamic set of skills that can be developed and refined. One effective way to enhance your emotional intelligence is through mindfulness practices, such as meditation and self-reflection. These practices can help you become more aware of your emotions and improve your ability to regulate them. Additionally, seeking feedback from others can provide valuable insights into your emotional strengths and areas for improvement.

Another strategy for developing emotional intelligence is to engage in active listening. This involves fully concentrating on the speaker, understanding their message, and responding thoughtfully. Active listening not only improves your empathy but also strengthens your relationships by showing others that you value and respect their perspectives.

You can also enhance your emotional intelligence by setting and pursuing personal and professional development goals. Whether it's learning new skills, seeking mentorship, or participating in emotional intelligence training programs, continuous growth and improvement are key to becoming more emotionally intelligent.

Incorporating emotional intelligence into your daily life can lead to significant benefits. In the workplace, emotionally intelligent individuals are often better leaders, team players, and communicators. They can manage stress more effectively, resolve conflicts efficiently, and inspire others to achieve their best. In personal relationships, emotional intelligence fosters deeper connections, greater understanding, and more meaningful interactions.

Consider the story of Maya Angelou, the renowned poet, and activist, whose emotional intelligence was evident in her ability to connect with and inspire people from all walks of life. Angelou's empathy, self-awareness, and powerful communication skills allowed her to touch hearts and minds, leaving a lasting legacy of compassion and wisdom.

Strategies to Improve Emotional Intelligence

Improving emotional intelligence (EI) involves refining the skills that enable us to understand and manage our own emotions, as well as those of others. This chapter provides practical strategies to enhance your emotional intelligence, which can lead to better relationships, improved decision-making, and greater overall well-being.

One of the most effective ways to improve emotional intelligence is through self-reflection. Taking time to reflect on your emotions, reactions, and interactions can help you gain insight into your emotional patterns and triggers. Journaling is a powerful tool for this purpose. By writing about your daily experiences and emotional responses, you can identify recurring themes and areas for improvement. For example, if you notice that you often feel frustrated during team meetings, you can explore the underlying causes and develop strategies to manage this emotion more effectively.

Another essential strategy is to practice mindfulness. Mindfulness involves being present in the moment and fully experiencing your thoughts and feelings without judgment. Regular mindfulness meditation can increase your awareness of your emotions and enhance your ability to regulate them. Even a few minutes of daily mindfulness practice can significantly improve your emotional intelligence. For instance, by focusing on your breath and observing your thoughts without reacting to them, you can develop greater emotional stability and resilience.

Developing empathy is also crucial for enhancing emotional intelligence. Empathy allows you to understand and share the feelings of others, fostering deeper connections and better communication. To cultivate empathy, practice active listening. When someone is speaking to you, give them your full attention, avoid interrupting, and reflect on what they are saying. This not only shows respect but also helps you understand their perspective more clearly. Additionally, putting yourself in others' shoes and imagining how they might feel in a given situation can strengthen your empathetic abilities.

Improving your emotional intelligence also involves enhancing your social skills. Effective communication, conflict resolution, and teamwork are all aspects of strong social skills. One way to develop these skills is to seek feedback from others. Ask colleagues, friends, or family members for honest feedback about your interactions and behavior. This can provide valuable insights into how you are perceived and areas where you can improve. Additionally, engaging in group activities or volunteering can provide opportunities to practice and refine your social skills in a supportive environment.

Another important strategy is to manage stress effectively. High levels of stress can impair your ability to think clearly, make decisions, and regulate your emotions. Developing healthy coping mechanisms is essential for maintaining emotional balance. Physical exercise, for example, is a proven stress reliever that also boosts mood and energy levels. Activities such as yoga, tai chi, or even a brisk walk can help reduce stress and improve your emotional well-being. Additionally, ensuring you get enough sleep, eat a balanced diet, and maintain a healthy work-life balance are critical for managing stress.

Setting personal development goals can also enhance your emotional intelligence. Identify specific areas where you want to improve, such as managing anger, developing patience, or improving your listening skills. Create a plan with actionable steps to achieve these goals. For example, if you want to improve your patience, you might practice deep breathing exercises when you feel impatient or set a goal to wait for a few seconds before responding during conversations. Tracking your progress and celebrating small victories can keep you motivated and focused on your development.

Reading literature that explores human emotions and relationships can also enhance your emotional intelligence. Novels, biographies, and even poetry can provide insights into the complexities of human emotions and behaviors. By immersing yourself in the stories and experiences of others, you can develop a deeper understanding of different perspectives and emotional responses. This can, in turn, improve your ability to empathize with others and navigate social interactions more effectively.

Engaging in emotional intelligence training programs or workshops can provide structured learning and opportunities to practice EI skills. These programs often include activities such as role-playing, group discussions, and self-assessment exercises that can help you develop a deeper understanding of emotional intelligence and how to apply it in various contexts. Look for programs that are evidence-based and led by experienced facilitators to ensure you gain the most benefit.

Practicing gratitude is another powerful strategy to enhance emotional intelligence. Regularly reflecting on the positive aspects of your life and expressing gratitude can improve your emotional well-being and foster a more positive outlook. Keeping a gratitude journal, where you write down things you are thankful for each day, can help shift your focus from negative to positive emotions. This practice can also enhance your relationships by encouraging you to appreciate and acknowledge the contributions of others.

Building resilience is also key to improving emotional intelligence. Resilience involves the ability to bounce back from setbacks and adapt to difficult situations. Developing a growth mindset, where you view challenges as opportunities for learning and growth, can enhance your resilience. Additionally, seeking support from friends, family, or a mentor can provide a valuable network of encouragement and advice during tough times. By building resilience, you can maintain emotional stability and continue to develop your emotional intelligence even in the face of adversity.

Lastly, developing emotional intelligence requires a commitment to continuous learning and improvement. Stay curious and open to new experiences and perspectives. Engage in lifelong learning by reading books, attending seminars, or taking courses related to emotional intelligence and personal development. By continually seeking to expand your knowledge and skills, you can keep your emotional intelligence sharp and adaptable to changing circumstances.

Managing Stress and Anxiety

Stress and anxiety are pervasive elements of modern life, affecting individuals across all demographics. Learning to manage these feelings effectively is crucial for maintaining overall well-being and achieving personal and professional success. Practical strategies and techniques can help you navigate through stressful and anxious moments, fostering resilience and emotional stability.

Understanding the root causes of stress and anxiety is the first step in managing them. Stress often arises from external pressures, such as work deadlines, financial concerns, or relationship problems. Conversely, anxiety tends to be more internal, characterized by excessive worry and fear about future events. By identifying what triggers your stress and anxiety, you can develop targeted strategies to address these issues.

Consider Sarah, a marketing manager who often feels overwhelmed by her workload. She realized that her stress peaks during project deadlines. By mapping out her stress triggers, she identified specific tasks that caused the most anxiety and began to explore ways to manage them better. This self-awareness is a critical component in the journey to managing stress and anxiety.

One effective strategy for managing stress and anxiety is practicing mindfulness. Mindfulness involves staying present in the moment and observing your thoughts and feelings without judgment. Techniques such as mindful breathing, meditation, and body scanning can help calm your mind and reduce stress. Mindfulness can be practiced anywhere—whether you're taking a walk, sitting at your desk, or lying in bed. Regular mindfulness practice has been shown to decrease anxiety and improve emotional regulation.

Physical exercise is another powerful tool in managing stress and anxiety. Regular physical activity releases endorphins, which are natural mood lifters. Exercise also helps reduce the levels of stress hormones, such as cortisol, in your body. Activities like running, swimming, yoga, and even brisk walking can make a significant difference. For example, John, a software engineer, found that starting his day with a 30-minute jog helped him stay focused and calm throughout his demanding workday.

Establishing a balanced routine can also mitigate stress and anxiety. This includes setting realistic goals, prioritizing tasks, and breaking them into manageable steps. Time management techniques, such as creating a to-do list or using a planner, can help you stay organized and reduce the feeling of being overwhelmed. Remember to schedule breaks and downtime to recharge. For instance, Emma, a medical student, uses the Pomodoro Technique, which involves studying for 25 minutes and then taking a 5-minute break. This method helps her maintain concentration and avoid burnout.

Social support plays a critical role in managing stress and anxiety. Sharing your feelings with friends, family, or a therapist can provide comfort and perspective. Engaging in social activities and building a support network can help you feel less isolated and more understood. Consider joining clubs, interest groups, or online communities where you can connect with others who share similar experiences. Mark, who struggled with anxiety, found solace in a local hiking group where he formed meaningful connections and enjoyed the therapeutic benefits of nature.

Developing healthy coping mechanisms is essential for managing stress and anxiety. This includes avoiding unhealthy habits such as smoking, excessive drinking, or overeating. Instead, find constructive outlets like engaging in hobbies, practicing relaxation techniques, or exploring creative activities. Rachel, an accountant, discovered that painting served as a perfect escape from her daily stresses, allowing her to express herself and unwind.

Adequate sleep is also vital in managing stress and anxiety. Poor sleep can exacerbate these feelings, creating a vicious cycle. Aim for 7-9 hours of quality sleep each night by establishing a consistent sleep routine. Create a calming bedtime ritual, such as reading, taking a warm bath, or practicing gentle yoga. Avoid screens and stimulating activities before bed to promote better sleep. Michael, a high school teacher, found that setting a regular sleep schedule and creating a relaxing pre-sleep routine significantly reduced his stress levels.

Nutrition plays a role in managing stress and anxiety as well. A balanced diet rich in fruits, vegetables, whole grains, and lean proteins can support overall health and improve your mood. Stay hydrated and limit caffeine and sugar intake, as these can increase anxiety levels. Maria, a nurse, noticed a marked improvement in her stress levels after incorporating more whole foods into her diet and cutting back on caffeinated beverages.

Learning to say no is another important aspect of managing stress and anxiety. Overcommitting yourself can lead to burnout and increased stress. Recognize your limits and prioritize your well-being by setting boundaries. Politely decline additional responsibilities or delegate tasks when necessary. James, a lawyer, found that by limiting his workload and setting clear boundaries, he could manage his stress more effectively and maintain a healthier work-life balance.

Cognitive-behavioral techniques can also be beneficial in managing stress and anxiety. This involves identifying and challenging negative thought patterns and replacing them with more positive and realistic ones. For example, if you find yourself thinking, "I can't handle this," try reframing it to, "This is challenging, but I can take it one step at a time." Cognitive restructuring can help you develop a more resilient mindset and reduce anxiety.

Seeking professional help is crucial when stress and anxiety become overwhelming or persistent. Therapists, counselors, and psychologists can provide valuable support and guidance. Therapeutic approaches such as cognitive-behavioral therapy (CBT), dialectical behavior therapy (DBT), and mindfulness-based stress reduction (MBSR) have proven effective in treating anxiety and stress-related disorders. Don't hesitate to reach out for professional help if needed. Sophie, who experienced chronic anxiety, found significant relief through regular sessions with a licensed therapist.

Engaging in relaxation techniques can also help manage stress and anxiety. Techniques such as deep breathing, progressive muscle relaxation, and visualization can calm your mind and body. Practice these techniques regularly to build resilience and reduce your stress response. David, a college student, incorporated deep breathing exercises into his daily routine, which helped him stay calm during exams and stressful situations.

Finally, it's important to maintain a positive outlook and practice self-compassion. Be kind to yourself and recognize that it's okay to make mistakes and experience setbacks. Celebrate your successes, no matter how small, and remind yourself of your strengths and achievements. Positive self-talk and affirmations can boost your confidence and reduce anxiety. Laura, a small business owner, found that by focusing on her accomplishments and practicing self-compassion, she could better manage the stresses of running her business.

Building Healthy Relationships

Healthy relationships are the cornerstone of a fulfilling life. They provide emotional support, companionship, and a sense of belonging. Whether these relationships are with family members, friends, or romantic partners, the principles of building and maintaining them remain consistent. Developing such relationships requires effort, understanding, and effective communication.

Consider the story of Anna and her best friend, Mark. Their friendship began in college and has endured many challenges over the years. Despite their different personalities, they have maintained a strong bond through mutual respect and open communication. Anna values Mark's honesty, even when it's difficult to hear, and Mark appreciates Anna's empathy and understanding. Their relationship exemplifies the importance of foundational values in building healthy connections.

Effective communication is the bedrock of any healthy relationship. It involves not only expressing your thoughts and feelings but also actively listening to the other person. Listening attentively shows that you value the other person's perspective. Practice reflective listening by repeating back what you heard in your own words, ensuring you understood correctly. For example, if your partner mentions feeling neglected, respond with, "So, you're feeling like I haven't been giving you enough attention lately?" This technique helps clarify misunderstandings and demonstrates empathy.

Trust is another critical element in building healthy relationships. It takes time to develop and can be easily broken, so it's essential to be consistent and reliable. Trust involves being honest, keeping promises, and respecting each other's boundaries. When trust is compromised, it requires sincere effort to rebuild. Sarah and Tom, a married couple, faced a breach of trust when Tom admitted to hiding financial troubles. Through open dialogue and counseling, they worked together to rebuild their trust, demonstrating that recovery is possible with commitment and honesty.

Conflict is inevitable in any relationship, but how you handle it can strengthen or weaken your bond. Approach conflicts with a problem-solving mindset rather than a confrontational one. Focus on the issue at hand without resorting to personal attacks. Use "I" statements to express how you feel, such as "I feel hurt when you cancel our plans last minute" instead of "You never keep your promises." This approach reduces defensiveness and promotes constructive dialogue.

Mutual respect is fundamental to healthy relationships. Respecting each other's opinions, feelings, and boundaries fosters a supportive environment. It's important to acknowledge and appreciate your differences rather than trying to change the other person. Celebrate each other's successes and be understanding during tough times. For example, when Emily's friend, Jake, received a promotion, she threw a small celebration to honor his achievement. This act of support strengthened their friendship and showed that Emily genuinely cared about Jake's happiness.

Spending quality time together is crucial for building healthy relationships. In today's fast-paced world, it's easy to get caught up in work and other commitments, but prioritizing time with loved ones is essential. Whether it's a weekly dinner, a weekend getaway, or just a phone call, regular interaction helps maintain a strong connection. Consider the example of Lily and her grandfather, who set aside Sunday afternoons for tea and conversation. These moments not only deepen their bond but also create lasting memories.

Shared interests and activities can also enhance your relationships. Engaging in hobbies or projects together provides opportunities for connection and collaboration. It can be as simple as cooking a meal, hiking, or working on a DIY project. Sam and his partner, Alex, discovered a mutual love for gardening, which became a meaningful way for them to spend time together and nurture their relationship.

Empathy is a powerful tool in building healthy relationships. It involves understanding and sharing the feelings of another person. When someone expresses joy, sadness, or frustration, try to imagine yourself in their position. This perspective-taking helps you respond with compassion and support. For instance, when Rachel confided in her friend about a difficult breakup, her friend listened without judgment and offered a comforting presence, making Rachel feel understood and supported.

Independence and space within a relationship are also important. While spending time together is crucial, it's equally important to maintain your individuality and personal interests. Encourage each other to pursue personal goals and hobbies. This balance of togetherness and independence can prevent feelings of suffocation and promote a healthier dynamic. Jane and Robert, a couple with demanding careers, support each other's professional and personal growth, ensuring they both have space to thrive individually while maintaining their strong connection.

Appreciation and gratitude go a long way in nurturing healthy relationships. Regularly expressing appreciation for each other reinforces positive feelings and strengthens your bond. Small acts of kindness, such as a thank you note or an unexpected gesture, can make a significant impact. Consider the case of Maria and her sister, who make it a habit to thank each other for even the smallest favors. This practice has made their relationship more positive and resilient over the years.

Setting and respecting boundaries is essential in any relationship. Boundaries define what is acceptable and what is not, helping to protect your well-being. Communicate your boundaries clearly and respect those of others. If someone crosses a boundary, address it calmly and assertively. For instance, if your friend frequently makes last-minute plans that disrupt your schedule, let them know how it affects you and suggest planning in advance. This approach helps maintain mutual respect and prevents resentment.

Forgiveness is a vital component in sustaining healthy relationships. Holding onto grudges can create distance and tension. Understand that everyone makes mistakes, and be willing to forgive and move forward. Letting go of past hurts can lead to healing and a stronger bond. When David's colleague apologized for a misunderstanding at work, David chose to forgive and focus on rebuilding their professional relationship, which ultimately improved their teamwork and productivity.

Finally, seeking professional help when needed can be beneficial. Therapy or counseling is not only for times of crisis; it can also provide tools and strategies for strengthening relationships. A trained professional can offer an objective perspective and help you navigate challenges more effectively. When Jennifer and her husband faced communication issues, they sought couples therapy, which provided them with valuable insights and techniques to improve their relationship.

The Connection Between Emotions and Well-being

Imagine waking up on a bright, sunny morning, feeling a sense of excitement and joy bubbling up within you. That feeling isn't just a fleeting moment; it has profound implications for your overall well-being. Emotions, whether positive or negative, play a crucial role in our mental and physical health. Understanding this connection can empower us to manage our emotions better and enhance our quality of life.

Emotions are complex responses to internal and external stimuli. They encompass a range of feelings, from happiness and love to anger and sadness. These emotional responses are not isolated events; they influence our thoughts, behaviors, and even physiological processes. For instance, when you're happy, your body releases endorphins and other "feel-good" chemicals that boost your mood and energy levels. Conversely, stress and anxiety can trigger the release of cortisol, a hormone that, in high levels, can lead to health issues like hypertension and weakened immune function.

Consider the story of John, a high-powered executive who constantly felt stressed and overwhelmed by his responsibilities. Despite his professional success, John's chronic stress began to take a toll on his health. He experienced frequent headaches, insomnia, and a weakened immune system. It wasn't until he started practicing mindfulness and emotional regulation techniques that he noticed significant improvements in his well-being. By learning to manage his emotional responses, John was able to reduce his stress levels, improve his sleep, and boost his overall health.

Mindfulness is a powerful tool for connecting with and understanding our emotions. It involves paying attention to the present moment without judgment. By observing our thoughts and feelings as they arise, we can gain insights into our emotional patterns and triggers. For example, if you notice that you feel anxious every time you check your work email, mindfulness can help you recognize this pattern and develop strategies to manage your anxiety. Techniques like deep breathing, meditation, and progressive muscle relaxation can help calm the mind and body, reducing the impact of negative emotions on your well-being.

Emotional intelligence (EQ) is another key factor in the connection between emotions and well-being. EQ involves the ability to recognize, understand, and manage our own emotions, as well as the emotions of others. High EQ is associated with better stress management, improved relationships, and greater overall happiness. Developing EQ starts with self-awareness—recognizing your emotional states and understanding their impact on your thoughts and behaviors. For instance, if you realize that you tend to lash out in anger when you're stressed, you can work on strategies to manage your stress more effectively and communicate more constructively.

Empathy, a component of EQ, allows us to connect with others on a deeper level. By understanding and sharing the feelings of others, we can build stronger, more supportive relationships. This social support is crucial for our well-being. Studies have shown that individuals with strong social connections have lower levels of anxiety and depression, higher self-esteem, and even longer lifespans. When we feel understood and supported by others, our emotional health flourishes, contributing to overall well-being.

Take the example of Emma, who, after moving to a new city, felt isolated and lonely. Her well-being suffered as she struggled to adjust to her new environment. By joining local clubs and engaging in community activities, Emma gradually built a network of supportive relationships. These connections provided her with emotional support, reducing her feelings of loneliness and enhancing her sense of belonging. Through empathy and social engagement, Emma was able to improve her emotional health and overall well-being.

Gratitude is another emotion that has a significant impact on well-being. Practicing gratitude involves recognizing and appreciating the positive aspects of our lives. Research has shown that individuals who regularly practice gratitude experience higher levels of happiness, reduced stress, and better physical health. Keeping a gratitude journal, where you write down things you're thankful for each day, can help cultivate a positive mindset. For example, expressing gratitude for a beautiful sunset, a kind gesture from a friend, or a personal achievement can shift your focus from negative to positive experiences, enhancing your emotional well-being.

Resilience, the ability to bounce back from adversity, is closely linked to emotional well-being. Resilient individuals are better equipped to handle stress and setbacks, maintaining a positive outlook even in challenging times. Building resilience involves developing coping strategies, such as seeking social support, practicing self-care, and maintaining a sense of purpose. Consider the story of Lisa, who faced a series of personal and professional setbacks. Instead of succumbing to despair, Lisa focused on her strengths, sought support from friends and family, and pursued activities that brought her joy. Her resilience helped her navigate through tough times and emerge stronger, with a renewed sense of well-being.

Physical activity is another important factor in the connection between emotions and well-being. Exercise has been shown to release endorphins, which act as natural mood lifters. Regular physical activity can reduce symptoms of depression and anxiety, improve sleep, and boost self-esteem. For example, running, yoga, or even a brisk walk can significantly improve your mood and energy levels. Incorporating physical activity into your daily routine can be a powerful way to enhance your emotional health and overall well-being.

Nutrition also plays a role in our emotional health. A balanced diet rich in fruits, vegetables, whole grains, and lean proteins provides the nutrients our brains need to function optimally. Certain foods, like those high in omega-3 fatty acids, have been shown to reduce symptoms of depression and anxiety. Conversely, a diet high in processed foods and sugar can negatively impact our mood and energy levels. Paying attention to what you eat can help regulate your emotions and improve your overall well-being.

Sleep is another critical factor that influences our emotions. Poor sleep can lead to irritability, mood swings, and increased stress levels. Prioritizing good sleep hygiene—such as maintaining a regular sleep schedule, creating a restful environment, and avoiding caffeine and electronic devices before bed—can improve the quality of your sleep and, in turn, your emotional health.

Finally, seeking professional help when needed is an important step in managing your emotions and well-being. Therapy or counseling can provide valuable tools and strategies for understanding and regulating your emotions. A mental health professional can offer support, guidance, and a safe space to explore your feelings. For example, cognitive-behavioral therapy (CBT) can help you identify and change negative thought patterns that contribute to emotional distress. By addressing underlying issues and developing healthy coping mechanisms, therapy can significantly enhance your emotional well-being.

Chapter 5

Physical Well-being and Personal Growth

The Importance of Physical Health in Personal Growth

On a brisk autumn morning, Lisa decided to take a walk through the park. She had recently committed to improving her physical health, believing it was the missing link in her journey toward personal growth. What she discovered was the profound impact that physical well-being had on her overall development. Physical health is not just about maintaining a fit body; it plays an essential role in our mental, emotional, and personal growth.

Physical health forms the foundation upon which personal growth is built. When our bodies are strong and functioning optimally, we have the energy and resilience to tackle life's challenges. Conversely, poor physical health can be a significant barrier to personal growth. Chronic illnesses, fatigue, and other health problems can sap our energy, making it difficult to focus on self-improvement and achieving our goals. For Lisa, the realization came when she noticed how much more productive and motivated she felt after incorporating regular exercise and a balanced diet into her routine.

Exercise is a cornerstone of physical health and has far-reaching benefits for personal growth. Regular physical activity improves cardiovascular health, strengthens muscles, and enhances flexibility. More importantly, it has a profound impact on mental health. Exercise stimulates the release of endorphins, which are natural mood lifters. It reduces symptoms of depression and anxiety, improves sleep quality, and boosts cognitive function. For instance, Lisa found that her morning runs not only helped her stay fit but also cleared her mind, allowing her to approach her work and personal projects with greater clarity and focus.

Nutrition is another critical component of physical health. A balanced diet provides the necessary nutrients that our bodies need to function effectively. Consuming a variety of fruits, vegetables, whole grains, lean proteins, and healthy fats supports optimal body and brain function. Poor nutrition, on the other hand, can lead to a host of health problems, including obesity, heart disease, and diabetes, which can impede personal growth. Lisa realized the impact of nutrition when she switched from a diet high in processed foods to one rich in whole, natural foods. She experienced increased energy levels, better concentration, and an overall improvement in her mood.

Sleep is often overlooked, yet it is crucial for physical health and personal growth. Quality sleep allows our bodies to repair and regenerate, and it is essential for cognitive function. Chronic sleep deprivation can lead to a range of health issues, including impaired memory, reduced focus, and increased stress levels. Establishing good sleep hygiene practices, such as maintaining a regular sleep schedule and creating a restful sleep environment, can significantly enhance physical and mental health. Lisa's commitment to going to bed at the same time each night and reducing screen time before bed resulted in more restful sleep and greater productivity during the day.

Stress management is another key aspect of physical health that directly impacts personal growth. Chronic stress can have detrimental effects on both physical and mental health, leading to issues such as hypertension, weakened immune function, and mental health disorders. Learning to manage stress through practices like mindfulness, meditation, and yoga can improve overall well-being. For Lisa, incorporating yoga into her daily routine helped her manage stress more effectively, allowing her to remain calm and focused even in challenging situations.

Building physical health also involves staying hydrated. Water is essential for nearly every bodily function, including digestion, temperature regulation, and joint lubrication. Dehydration can lead to fatigue, headaches, and impaired cognitive function. By making a conscious effort to drink adequate water throughout the day, Lisa noticed a significant improvement in her energy levels and overall sense of well-being.

The role of physical health in personal growth extends beyond individual practices. It also involves understanding the importance of preventive healthcare. Regular check-ups, screenings, and vaccinations can help detect and prevent health issues before they become serious problems. By taking a proactive approach to her health, Lisa was able to catch potential issues early and address them, ensuring that they did not impede her personal growth journey.

Social connections and physical health are also closely linked. Engaging in physical activities with others, such as joining a sports team or a fitness class, can provide both physical and social benefits. Strong social connections have been shown to improve mental health, reduce stress, and increase longevity. For Lisa, joining a local running club not only helped her stay active but also allowed her to build a supportive network of like-minded individuals who encouraged and motivated her.

Another important aspect of physical health is maintaining a healthy weight. Obesity can lead to numerous health problems, including diabetes, heart disease, and joint issues, which can hinder personal growth. Achieving and maintaining a healthy weight through a combination of diet and exercise can improve overall health and increase self-esteem. Lisa's journey to a healthier weight involved setting realistic goals, tracking her progress, and celebrating her achievements, which boosted her confidence and sense of accomplishment.

Physical health also influences our ability to set and achieve goals. When we are physically healthy, we have the energy and mental clarity needed to set ambitious goals and work towards them. Poor health, on the other hand, can create obstacles that make it difficult to stay motivated and focused. Lisa found that as her physical health improved, she was better able to set and achieve personal and professional goals, leading to a greater sense of fulfillment and purpose.

The connection between physical health and personal growth is evident in the way our bodies and minds are interconnected. Physical activity, nutrition, sleep, stress management, hydration, preventive healthcare, social connections, and maintaining a healthy weight all contribute to our overall well-being. By prioritizing physical health, we create a solid foundation for personal growth, enabling us to reach our full potential.

Lisa's journey is a testament to the transformative power of physical health in personal growth. Through regular exercise, a balanced diet, quality sleep, stress management, and social engagement, she was able to enhance her physical and mental well-being, paving the way for continuous personal development. By taking proactive steps to improve physical health, anyone can unlock their potential for personal growth and lead a more fulfilling and purposeful life.

Nutrition and Its Impact on Well-being

Anna had always thought that nutrition was a complex science reserved for dietitians and health experts. But after months of feeling sluggish and unmotivated, she began to suspect that her diet might be playing a significant role in her overall well-being. She decided to take a closer look at what she was eating and discovered a world where food was not just fuel, but a powerful tool for enhancing her physical and mental health.

Nutrition is the cornerstone of well-being. The food we consume provides the essential nutrients our bodies need to function effectively. Carbohydrates, proteins, fats, vitamins, and minerals each play unique roles in maintaining health and vitality. When our diet is balanced and nutrient-rich, we feel more energetic, think more clearly, and are better equipped to handle stress. Conversely, poor nutrition can lead to a myriad of health issues, from chronic diseases to mental health disorders, which can significantly impact our quality of life.

Carbohydrates are the body's primary source of energy. They are found in foods like grains, fruits, vegetables, and legumes. While some carbohydrates, such as those found in whole grains and vegetables, provide sustained energy and are rich in fiber, others, like refined sugars, can cause energy spikes and crashes. Anna found that by switching from sugary snacks to whole grain options, she experienced more stable energy levels throughout the day, which improved her productivity and mood.

Proteins are the building blocks of our body. They are essential for repairing tissues, building muscles, and supporting immune function. Good sources of protein include meat, fish, eggs, dairy products, legumes, and nuts. For those who follow a plant-based diet, combining different plant proteins can ensure they get all the essential amino acids. Anna began incorporating a variety of protein sources into her meals, from eggs at breakfast to beans and lentils at dinner, and noticed a significant improvement in her muscle tone and overall strength.

Fats are another crucial component of a healthy diet. They provide energy, support cell growth, protect organs, and keep the body warm. However, not all fats are created equal. Unsaturated fats, found in foods like avocados, nuts, and olive oil, are beneficial and can help reduce the risk of heart disease. Saturated and trans fats, found in fried foods and baked goods, should be consumed in moderation as they can increase the risk of cardiovascular problems. By replacing unhealthy fats with healthier options, Anna was able to improve her cholesterol levels and feel more vibrant.

Vitamins and minerals are micronutrients that play vital roles in nearly every bodily function. Vitamins such as A, C, D, E, and the B-complex group are essential for immune function, energy production, and skin health, among other things. Minerals like calcium, potassium, and magnesium are crucial for bone health, nerve function, and muscle contraction. A diet rich in a variety of fruits, vegetables, whole grains, and lean proteins can help ensure we get the necessary vitamins and minerals. Anna began to diversify her diet to include more colorful fruits and vegetables, which not only made her meals more enjoyable but also boosted her overall health.

Hydration is another key aspect of nutrition that is often overlooked. Water is essential for digestion, nutrient absorption, and temperature regulation. Dehydration can lead to fatigue, headaches, and impaired cognitive function. Anna made a conscious effort to drink more water throughout the day, carrying a reusable bottle with her wherever she went.

This simple change had a profound impact on her energy levels and mental clarity.

The timing of meals can also affect well-being. Eating at regular intervals helps maintain stable blood sugar levels, which can prevent energy crashes and overeating. Skipping meals, on the other hand, can lead to increased hunger and poor food choices later in the day. Anna started to prioritize regular, balanced meals and snacks, which helped her maintain consistent energy levels and avoid late-night cravings.

Mindful eating is another practice that can enhance well-being. It involves paying attention to the sensory experience of eating, noticing the flavors, textures, and smells of food, and recognizing hunger and fullness cues. By slowing down and savoring her meals, Anna found that she enjoyed her food more and felt satisfied with smaller portions. This not only helped her maintain a healthy weight but also reduced stress around eating.

The relationship between nutrition and mental health is also significant. Certain nutrients, such as omega-3 fatty acids, B vitamins, and antioxidants, play a crucial role in brain function and mental health. Foods rich in these nutrients, such as fatty fish, nuts, seeds, and leafy greens, can help reduce symptoms of depression and anxiety. Anna began to include more brain-boosting foods in her diet and noticed an improvement in her mood and cognitive function.

Gut health is another important aspect of nutrition that impacts well-being. The gut microbiome, a complex community of microorganisms living in the digestive tract, plays a crucial role in digestion, immune function, and even mood regulation. A diet high in fiber, fermented foods, and probiotics can support a healthy gut microbiome. Anna discovered the benefits of incorporating foods like yogurt, kefir, sauerkraut, and whole grains into her diet, which improved her digestion and overall health.

Cultural and personal preferences also play a role in nutrition. It's important to find a balanced diet that is enjoyable and sustainable. Anna experimented with different cuisines and recipes, incorporating her favorite flavors and ingredients while maintaining a focus on nutrient-dense foods. This approach made healthy eating a pleasurable and integral part of her lifestyle rather than a chore.

Addressing food accessibility and affordability is also crucial for improving nutrition and well-being. Not everyone has access to fresh, healthy foods, and socioeconomic factors can significantly impact dietary choices. Community programs, education, and support can help make nutritious foods more accessible to everyone. Anna became involved in local initiatives to promote healthy eating in her community, realizing that collective efforts can make a significant difference in public health.

Nutrition is a dynamic and individualized journey. What works for one person may not work for another, and it often requires experimentation and adjustments. Anna kept a food journal to track her meals and how they made her feel, which helped her identify patterns and make informed choices. This personalized approach allowed her to create a diet that supported her unique needs and goals.

The Benefits of Regular Exercise

John had always led a fairly sedentary lifestyle, spending most of his day behind a desk and his evenings in front of the television. He often felt sluggish and found himself short of breath after climbing just a few stairs. A visit to his physician revealed that his cholesterol levels were high, and he was at risk for developing heart disease. Determined to turn his life around, John embarked on a journey to incorporate regular exercise into his routine. Little did he know that this decision would transform not only his physical health but also his mental and emotional well-being.

The benefits of regular exercise are vast and well-documented. Engaging in physical activity can lead to significant improvements in cardiovascular health. Regular exercise strengthens the heart muscle, enhances its efficiency in pumping blood, and helps maintain healthy blood pressure levels. John started with brisk walking, gradually increasing his pace and distance. Within a few months, he noticed that he could climb stairs without losing his breath, and his blood pressure readings were consistently lower.

Weight management is another critical benefit of regular exercise. Physical activity helps burn calories and build muscle mass, which in turn boosts metabolism. For those looking to lose weight, combining exercise with a balanced diet can lead to sustainable weight loss. John incorporated a mix of aerobic exercises, like jogging and cycling, with strength training to build muscle. This combination not only helped him shed excess pounds but also improved his overall body composition, giving him a leaner and more toned physique.

Mental health benefits are equally significant. Exercise has been shown to reduce symptoms of depression and anxiety, improve mood, and enhance overall mental well-being. The release of endorphins during physical activity acts as a natural mood lifter. John, who had struggled with bouts of anxiety, found that regular exercise provided him with a much-needed outlet for stress relief. The rhythmic nature of running and the focus required in weightlifting helped him clear his mind and feel more centered.

Moreover, exercise can boost cognitive function and reduce the risk of cognitive decline as we age. Physical activity increases blood flow to the brain, promoting the growth of new neurons and improving brain plasticity. John noticed that his concentration and memory improved, which had a positive impact on his productivity at work. He found that his ability to solve problems and think creatively was enhanced, likely due to the mental clarity that came with regular physical activity.

Another benefit of regular exercise is improved sleep quality. Physical activity can help regulate sleep patterns and reduce the time it takes to fall asleep. John, who often struggled with insomnia, began to experience deeper and more restful sleep. His energy levels during the day improved, and he no longer felt the need for afternoon naps or excessive caffeine to stay awake.

Regular exercise also strengthens the immune system, making the body more resilient to infections and illnesses. Physical activity promotes good circulation, which allows immune cells to move more freely throughout the body, increasing their ability to detect and fight off pathogens. John found that he fell sick less frequently and recovered more quickly from minor ailments, such as colds and flu.

Social benefits should not be overlooked either. Engaging in group activities or joining a fitness class can provide a sense of community and support. John joined a local running club, where he met new friends who shared similar fitness goals. The camaraderie and mutual encouragement he experienced in this group setting motivated him to stay consistent with his exercise routine.

Flexibility and balance also improve with regular exercise, which is particularly important as we age. Activities like yoga and Pilates enhance core strength, flexibility, and stability, reducing the risk of falls and injuries. John, who had previously suffered from occasional back pain, found that incorporating yoga into his routine helped alleviate his discomfort and improved his overall posture and balance.

The benefits of exercise extend to chronic disease management as well. Regular physical activity can help manage conditions such as diabetes, arthritis, and high cholesterol. Exercise improves insulin sensitivity, which is crucial for managing blood sugar levels in individuals with diabetes. For those with arthritis, low-impact activities like swimming and cycling can reduce pain and improve joint function. John, with his improved cholesterol levels, exemplified how exercise can be a powerful tool in managing and even reversing certain health conditions.

One often overlooked benefit of regular exercise is its impact on longevity. Studies have shown that individuals who engage in regular physical activity tend to live longer and have a lower risk of premature death. Exercise helps maintain healthy body weight, reduces inflammation, and improves cardiovascular health, all of which contribute to a longer, healthier life. John felt more vibrant and alive than he had in years, and he looked forward to many more active years ahead.

The journey to incorporating regular exercise into one's life can start small. John began with short walks around his neighborhood, gradually increasing the duration and intensity of his workouts. He set realistic goals and tracked his progress, celebrating each milestone along the way. Over time, exercise became a natural and enjoyable part of his daily routine.

It's essential to find activities that you enjoy and that fit into your lifestyle. Whether it's dancing, hiking, swimming, or playing a sport, the key is to stay active and make it a habit. John discovered a love for running and weightlifting, which kept him motivated and excited about his fitness journey.

Staying consistent is crucial for reaping the long-term benefits of exercise. John learned to listen to his body, allowing for rest and recovery when needed, but he also pushed himself to stay disciplined and committed. He found that having a workout buddy or joining a fitness group helped him stay accountable and consistent.

Proper nutrition and hydration are also vital components of an effective exercise regimen. John paid attention to his diet, ensuring he fueled his body with the right nutrients to support his workouts. He stayed hydrated, especially before and after exercise, to maintain optimal performance and recovery.

Sleep and Restoration

Emily had always been a night owl, often staying up late to binge-watch her favorite TV shows or scroll through social media. She would drag herself out of bed each morning, feeling groggy and irritable. The lack of quality sleep began to take a toll on her health and productivity. Desperate for a change, Emily decided to prioritize sleep and restoration, embarking on a journey that would revolutionize her well-being.

Sleep is an essential function that allows our body and mind to recharge, leaving us refreshed and alert when we wake up. Without adequate sleep, our cognitive functions, mood, and physical health suffer. For Emily, understanding the stages of sleep was the first step in appreciating its importance. Sleep is divided into two main types: rapid eye movement (REM) and non-REM sleep. Each type plays a critical role in maintaining our health.

Non-REM sleep consists of three stages. The first stage is light sleep, where we drift in and out of consciousness. The second stage is a deeper sleep, where our body temperature drops and heart rate slows. The third stage, known as deep sleep, is the most restorative. During deep sleep, tissue growth and repair occur, energy is restored, and essential hormones are released. REM sleep, on the other hand, is when most dreaming occurs. This stage is crucial for cognitive functions such as memory consolidation, learning, and emotional regulation.

Emily learned that poor sleep hygiene was one of the reasons for her restless nights. Sleep hygiene refers to habits and practices that promote consistent, uninterrupted sleep. To improve her sleep hygiene, Emily made several changes to her routine. She established a regular sleep schedule, going to bed and waking up at the same time every day, even on weekends. This consistency helped regulate her internal clock, making it easier to fall asleep and wake up naturally.

Creating a relaxing bedtime routine was another significant step. Emily began winding down an hour before bed, engaging in calming activities such as reading a book, taking a warm bath, or practicing gentle yoga. She also made her bedroom a sleep-friendly environment by keeping it cool, dark, and quiet. Investing in a comfortable mattress and pillows made a noticeable difference in her sleep quality.

Limiting exposure to screens before bedtime was crucial. The blue light emitted by phones, tablets, and computers can interfere with the production of melatonin, the hormone that regulates sleep. Emily set a rule to avoid screens at least an hour before bed, opting for more relaxing activities instead. She also used blue light filters on her devices to reduce their impact when she did need to use them at night.

Diet and exercise play a significant role in sleep health. Emily discovered that consuming large meals, caffeine, or alcohol close to bedtime disrupted her sleep. She started eating her last meal at least two hours before bed and avoided caffeine in the afternoon and evening. Regular exercise, particularly aerobic activity, helped her fall asleep faster and enjoy deeper sleep. However, she made sure to finish any vigorous exercise at least a few hours before bedtime, as it can be stimulating.

Stress and anxiety can wreak havoc on sleep. Emily incorporated stress-reduction techniques into her daily routine to calm her mind before bed. Practices such as mindfulness meditation, deep breathing exercises, and keeping a gratitude journal helped her manage stress and let go of worries that might keep her awake at night.

Understanding the consequences of sleep deprivation reinforced Emily's commitment to better sleep. Chronic sleep deprivation can lead to a host of health problems, including weakened immunity, increased risk of chronic conditions like heart disease and diabetes, weight gain, and impaired cognitive function. Emily realized that prioritizing sleep was not just about feeling rested but also about protecting her long-term health.

The link between sleep and mental health is profound. Poor sleep can exacerbate symptoms of mental health conditions such as depression and anxiety, while good sleep can improve mood and emotional resilience. Emily noticed that as her sleep improved, so did her overall outlook on life. She felt more positive, patient, and better equipped to handle daily challenges.

One of the most surprising benefits Emily experienced was enhanced cognitive function. Adequate sleep improved her attention, problem-solving skills, and creativity. She found that tasks that once seemed daunting were now manageable, and her productivity soared. Her memory also improved, making it easier to retain new information and recall details.

Sleep also plays a crucial role in weight management. Lack of sleep disrupts the balance of hormones that control hunger and appetite, leading to increased cravings and overeating. By getting sufficient rest, Emily found it easier to make healthy food choices and maintain a balanced diet. She also had more energy to stay active, which further supported her weight management goals.

The impact of sleep on physical performance cannot be overstated. Adequate rest allows muscles to recover and grow, improves coordination, and enhances overall physical endurance. Emily, who enjoyed running, noticed that her performance improved significantly with better sleep. She could run longer distances with less fatigue, and her recovery time shortened.

Social interactions also benefited from Emily's improved sleep. She was more engaged, attentive, and empathetic, strengthening her relationships with friends and family. Good sleep made her more resilient to social stressors and better equipped to navigate conflicts.

For those struggling with sleep, it's important to recognize when professional help is needed. Sleep disorders such as insomnia, sleep apnea, and restless legs syndrome require medical attention. Emily sought advice from a sleep specialist when she noticed persistent issues despite making lifestyle changes. The specialist conducted a sleep study and provided personalized recommendations that further improved her sleep quality.

Emily's journey to better sleep and restoration highlights the profound impact that sleep has on every aspect of our lives. By prioritizing sleep, we can enhance our physical health, mental well-being, and overall quality of life. Small changes in our daily habits and routines can lead to significant improvements in sleep, allowing us to wake up each day feeling refreshed and ready to take on the world.

Creating a Healthy Lifestyle Routine

Linda had always admired those who seemed to have their lives perfectly balanced, juggling work, family, and fitness with apparent ease. For years, she struggled to create a routine that allowed her to thrive rather than just survive. It wasn't until she decided to commit to a comprehensive approach to her well-being that she began to see real, lasting changes. Creating a healthy lifestyle routine became her goal, and the transformation was nothing short of remarkable.

The first step Linda took was to assess her current habits and identify areas that needed improvement. She kept a journal for a week, noting her eating patterns, physical activity, sleep quality, and stress levels. This self-assessment provided a clear picture of where she was starting and highlighted specific areas that required attention. Linda realized that her diet was inconsistent, her exercise sporadic, and her sleep often insufficient.

Establishing a balanced diet was a cornerstone of Linda's new routine. She learned that a nutritious diet should include a variety of foods to ensure she was getting all the necessary vitamins and minerals. Linda began planning her meals around whole foods, incorporating plenty of fruits, vegetables, lean proteins, whole grains, and healthy fats. She discovered the benefits of meal prepping, which saved time and helped her avoid the temptation of unhealthy snacks and fast food.

Hydration also became a priority. Linda started carrying a water bottle with her everywhere and set reminders to drink water throughout the day. Staying well-hydrated improved her energy levels and mental clarity, making it easier to stick to her new routine.

Physical activity was another essential component of Linda's healthy lifestyle. She realized that finding activities she enjoyed was key to maintaining a consistent exercise routine. Linda experimented with various forms of exercise, including yoga, swimming, and hiking, before settling on a mix that kept her engaged. She aimed for at least 150 minutes of moderate aerobic activity each week, along with strength training exercises twice a week.

To ensure she stayed motivated, Linda set specific, achievable goals. She signed up for a 5K race, which gave her a clear target to work towards. Tracking her progress using a fitness app provided a sense of accomplishment and helped her stay accountable. Linda also found that working out with friends made exercise more enjoyable and provided additional motivation.

Sleep hygiene was another critical area Linda focused on. She established a regular sleep schedule, going to bed and waking up at the same time each day. Creating a bedtime routine helped signal to her body that it was time to wind down. Linda avoided screens before bed, opting for relaxing activities like reading or taking a warm bath. Ensuring her bedroom was a comfortable, dark, and cool environment also contributed to better sleep quality.

Managing stress was essential for maintaining her new healthy lifestyle. Linda incorporated mindfulness practices into her daily routine, such as meditation and deep breathing exercises. These practices helped her stay present and reduce anxiety. She also made time for hobbies and activities that brought her joy, whether it was painting, gardening, or simply spending time with loved ones.

Linda discovered that setting realistic expectations was crucial. She accepted that not every day would go perfectly and that setbacks were a natural part of the process. Instead of getting discouraged, she focused on the progress she had made and reminded herself of her long-term goals. Celebrating small victories, like sticking to her meal plan for a week or completing a challenging workout, kept her motivated.

Building a healthy lifestyle routine also involved creating a supportive environment. Linda surrounded herself with people who encouraged her new habits and avoided those who undermined her efforts. She joined online communities and local groups where she could share her experiences and learn from others on similar journeys. Having a support network made a significant difference in her ability to stay on track.

Time management was another skill Linda honed. She learned to prioritize her health by scheduling workouts, meal prep, and relaxation time just as she would any other important appointment. Linda became more efficient with her tasks, which freed up time for her self-care activities. She also learned to say no to commitments that didn't align with her goals, ensuring she had the time and energy to focus on what mattered most.

Linda's journey to creating a healthy lifestyle routine taught her the importance of balance. She understood that an all-or-nothing approach was not sustainable. Instead, she aimed for progress, not perfection. Linda allowed herself occasional indulgences without guilt, knowing that a single treat wouldn't derail her overall efforts. This balanced approach made her new lifestyle enjoyable and sustainable.

As Linda continued to follow her routine, she noticed significant improvements in her overall well-being. Her energy levels increased, she felt more focused and productive, and her moods stabilized. Her physical health improved, with better fitness levels and a stronger immune system. Linda's self-confidence grew as she realized she had the power to take control of her health and well-being.

Creating a healthy lifestyle routine also had a positive impact on Linda's relationships. She became more present and engaged with her family and friends. Her new habits inspired those around her to make healthier choices, creating a ripple effect of positive change. Linda found that she had more patience and resilience, which improved her interactions and reduced conflicts.

Linda's story demonstrates that creating a healthy lifestyle routine is a journey that requires commitment, self-awareness, and perseverance. It's about making gradual, sustainable changes rather than seeking quick fixes. By focusing on balanced nutrition, regular physical activity, quality sleep, stress management, and a supportive environment, anyone can transform their health and well-being.

The key is to start small and build on successes. Identify areas for improvement, set realistic goals, and celebrate progress along the way. Surround yourself with supportive people and stay flexible, adapting your routine as needed. Remember that setbacks are part of the process and use them as learning opportunities rather than reasons to give up.